Peter Paul Galligan

Gary,

Best Wishes

Kevin

I dedicate this book to my wife, Anne,
and my two daughters, Sophie and Grace

About the Author

Kevin Galligan is the grandson of Peter Paul Galligan. He was born in January 1967, one month after the death of his grandfather. On reading his grandfather's historical letters, he was compelled to tell Peter Paul Galligan's story and his commitment to Irish freedom. His main sources of information for this book were Peter Paul Galligan's letters, files sourced at the National Archives in the UK, Bureau of Military History in Dublin, National Archives, Dublin and the University College Dublin archives.

Kevin is Regional Director of DX Ireland – a logistics operator specialising in the delivery of time sensitive and mission critical items. He lives in Dublin and is married with two children.

PETER PAUL GALLIGAN

'One of the Most Dangerous Men in the Rebel Movement'

Kevin Galligan

The Liffey Press

Published by
The Liffey Press Ltd
Raheny Shopping Centre, Second Floor
Raheny, Dublin 5, Ireland
www.theliffeypress.com

A catalogue record of this book is
available from the British Library.

ISBN 978-1-908308-20-7

Printed by the MPG Books Group

Contents

Preface

The stories of the prominent political figures that featured during the period 1916 to 1922 have been told several times by many authors. However, many of the men and women that took part in the Easter Rising and the War of Independence were equally devoted, but their stories have not been told. My grandfather, Peter Paul Galligan was deeply committed to achieving independence for Ireland and suffered greatly in order that the citizens of the Republic of Ireland could enjoy their democratic freedom.

My journey to write this book began in 2008 and continued until 2012. My main source of information was Peter Paul Galligan's letters, files sourced at the National Archives in the UK, Bureau of Military History in Dublin and the University College Dublin archives.

Paul Galligan dedicated most of his twenties and early thirties to the cause of Irish freedom. He was one of a generation of Irishmen and women that largely realised a centuries-long dream of Irish self-determination.

Galligan and his comrades in the Volunteers and the IRA thought of themselves as soldiers. They armed themselves, organised in military structures and carried out armed operations.

At the same time, this book is not intended to be an endorsement of political violence. The use of force always has it costs in terms of death and human suffering and this telling of Paul Galligan's life as a revolutionary is not an attempt to glorify the use of violence.

In the twenty-first century, it is to be hoped that anyone seeking radical change in Ireland and elsewhere can find non-violent ways of doing it. The Irish example of armed struggle attracted much interest throughout the colonised world but there are other methods of taking on entrenched power structures. Mahatma Gandhi brought the British Empire to the negotiating table through passive resistance and the communist regimes of Eastern Europe collapsed before popular protest in 1989 almost without a shot being fired.

I would like to thank my father, Liam Galligan (RIP) for providing the early inspiration for this book. My thanks to Colm Galligan for his contributions and to Mairin Dillon (nee Galligan) for access to Peter Paul Galligan's personal letters.

Many public civil servants were of great assistance to me during my research phase. The staff of the National Archives in the UK were always generous with their time and patience as I hogged the photocopier during the last 15 minutes of opening time. Thanks to the staff at the Military Archives in Rathmines for their quick response to so many requests. My gratitude to Fiona and Des in Mountjoy Prison who kindly sourced records for me.

Fionan O'Connell and Diarmuid Clifford came to my rescue when I needed translations from Irish in to English. Many thanks to Paula White who transcribed Paul Galligan's letters from dictaphone to electronic copy.

Colonel Tony McCourt, Military Judge, Defence Forces Ireland very kindly guided me through the court-martial process.

Thanks also to Anne-Marie Ryan in Kilmainham Jail, James Stevenson in Lincolnshire Archives, Lisa Spurrier of the Berkshire Record Office, Henry Goff in Enniscorthy, Gráinne Doran of Wexford County Council, staff of Cavan Library and National Archives in Dublin.

My sister, Aislinn Galligan kindly proof-read and corrected all those embarrassing typos and jumbled sentences.

Preface

Thanks to Michael McLoughlin and Eoin Purcell for their advice and introducing me to John Dorney.

My first version of this book was something similar to a history text book. However, my editor, John Dorney, brought my manuscript to life. His knowledge of this period was essential as he placed Paul Galligan's experiences in the context of the times. He brought new and fresh perspectives and took my manuscript and turned it in to a readable story.

But most importantly, I want to thank my family and particularly my wife Anne. Writing this book absorbed my personal time and involved many late nights and weekends, as I attempted to juggle work (which requires long hours anyway) along with family time and book time. Anne was full of encouragement and praise while my daughter Sophie (8) was very excited to hear about her great-grandfather's struggle for Irish freedom. The bedtime story about the princess who married the prince and lived happily ever after was often substituted for Galligan the Freedom Fighter. Even my youngest daughter, Grace (3) could sense the excitement.

Lastly, my sincere thanks to my brother, Paul Galligan, for generously providing finanical assistance towards the publication of this book.

Kevin Galligan
April 2012

Introduction

Paul Galligan is remembered by his family as an honourable man. He was 'very fair' and 'highly respected' by those who knew him. He 'never lost his temper', and enjoyed taking his sons to watch rugby matches at Castleknock Secondary School and Bective Rangers. A kind man, but not recalled as affectionate. His children remembered that he was a 'quiet man', who 'spoke very little about the past'.

Galligan had, since the 1930s, lived in Churchtown, south Dublin and he ran a successful men's outfitters on Henry Street, along with a warehousing business in central Dublin until his death in 1966, aged 78.[1]

At first glance, he appears to be an unexceptional member of his generation in Ireland – unusual only in that his hard work and business acumen enabled him to thrive in his own country and not emigrate like so many of his contemporaries.

A look at his funeral in 1966, however, reveals another side to the man, one he talked little about in his later years. Among the mourners were the President Éamon de Valera, former Taoiseach Seán Lemass and Seán MacEoin, former commander in chief of the Irish Army. The current Taoiseach Jack Lynch was represented by his private secretary. Galligan's coffin was accompanied to the graveyard at Deansgrange by a military escort and the casket was draped in the Irish tricolour.

The quiet businessman had once been a revolutionary. In his youth, Peter Paul Galligan had struggled alongside de Valera, Lemass and MacEoin for Irish independence.

In 1910, when most Irish people were still prepared to accept the compromise of Home Rule, he had joined the Irish Republican Brotherhood – dedicated to the foundation of an Irish Republic. In 1916 he commanded the Irish Volunteers in Enniscorthy, who during the Easter Rising flew the republican flag over Enniscorthy until they received the order from Dublin to surrender.

Éamon de Valera, as he watched the burial of Galligan, may have been thinking of the time when he and Galligan, imprisoned together in an English jail, refused to do prison work on principle, or when they and their comrades marched together out of the prison gates singing the Fenian anthem, 'God Save Ireland'.

Galligan had suffered severely for his principles. In 1916 he was sentenced to death for his part in the Rising. He was imprisoned on four occasions by the British for extended periods – despite having been elected as an MP in 1918. At times he had been put in solitary confinement and reduced to a diet of bread and water. He was shot and seriously wounded by British forces while in command of the IRA in his native Cavan in 1920, and suffered the accumulating stress and worry of being on the run. The rigours of guerrilla war and imprisonment brought him to the very edge of mental exhaustion and collapse.

The presence of both senior pro- and anti-Treaty figures at his funeral in MacEoin, de Valera and Lemass also tells us something. As a member of Dáil Eireann, Galligan voted for the Anglo-Irish Treaty in early 1922 but took an ambiguous stance in the following Civil War. He remained close to figures on both sides of the Treaty split and later became a director of the Fianna Fáil-inclined newspaper, *The Irish Press*.

By any standards, Paul Galligan was one of the most prominent in the generation of Irish people who helped to found the modern Irish state. He became involved in the separatist movement before the vast majority of his contemporaries and operated close to the highest levels of nationalist organisations, both political and military. He was recognised by his adversaries as a dangerous enemy. His Dublin Castle Intelligence file records that, 'he is considered one of the most dangerous men in the rebel movement'.[2]

If he spoke little in later life about the events of his youth, this may have been to try to forget the more traumatic aspects of the period. But his story still deserves to be told. This is an attempt at telling it.

Endnotes

[1] Colm Galligan, notes compiled on Peter Paul Galligan.

[2] Dublin Castle File no 88, Peter Paul Galligan, WO-35-207.

Chapter 1

The Making of an Irish Rebel, 1888-1913

'Where the sun sets on the mountains of Leitrim'

Peter Paul Galligan was born in Carrigallen, County Leitrim on 20 June 1888 – the son of Peter and Sarah (née O'Reilly) Galligan. To distinguish him from his father, Peter Paul was always known in the family simply as Paul.

Paul Galligan was the third of four sons, preceded by Eugene and Michael and followed by Jimmy. Tragedy marked the Galligan family when Paul was still very young as his mother Sarah died suddenly in tragic circumstances.[1] Paul's brother Michael also died tragically at the age of 21 after receiving a kick from a horse.

Not long after Sarah's death, Peter Galligan moved the family some 20 kilometres over the county border to his native Drumnalaragh in County Cavan where Paul was raised. Drumnalaragh was a rural townland in the parish of Ballinagh – without a village but supporting several family farms. According to the 1901 census, the area was inhabited by nine households, including three families of Galligans.[2] It may well have been for the support of these relatives in raising his sons in the absence of their mother, that Peter moved the family back there.

The land around Drumnalaragh is, like much of Cavan, interspersed with small hills or drumlins, with the result that

1

the landscape is broken up into many small green valleys. Overlooking the townland to the east are the hills of Ardkill Beg and Ardkill More, rising to a height of about 200 metres. Slightly further to the east is Slieve Gleh, a round grassy hump of 320 metres. Visible to the west are the higher hills in Leitrim.

The area is drained to the south and west by the River Erne, meaning that, unlike much of Cavan and Leitrim its valleys are not interspersed with many small lakes.

Paul Galligan clearly loved the countryside of his native place. In Lewes prison in 1917, his mind would wander back to the hills of Cavan and Leitrim. He wrote to his brother Eugene that at sunset he would, 'gaze to where the sun has set on a distant horizon and I follow it until I see it setting behind the Leitrim mountains, just as I used to watch it set at home'.[3]

Peter Galligan was a surveyor by trade, but also ran a farm in which he raised and sold cattle. He clearly passed on to Paul his business skills and attention to detail. Letters between the two men in later years are full of details of meticulously pre-pared personal accounts, debts to be settled and collected. The ability to organise and plan in this way no doubt helped Paul to rise within the IRB and the Volunteers, as well as subse-quently in his business career.

After attending national school, Paul Galligan went to St. Patrick's College, in Cavan town as a boarder. St. Patricks was a secondary school for Catholic boys, intended primarily to prepare bright boys for the seminary. Attendance at St. Pat-rick's meant paying a small fee – showing that the Galligans were, if not well-off, then at least financially secure.

Eugene, the eldest Galligan brother, with whom Paul kept up an extensive correspondence, also attended St. Patrick's, went on to become a priest and was stationed in Australia. While imprisoned after the Easter Rising, Paul, in a letter to Eugene quipped, 'How we would laugh a few years ago if someone said, "what a difference in these two brothers, one is destined for the Church and the other for the prison".'[4]

A Nationalist Education

Some accounts of the Irish revolutionary period stress the importance of Catholic, nationalist education in creating future rebels, but Paul Galligan remarked later of St. Patrick's only that the 'Irish [language] was taught here but as a subject only'.[5] Several other future IRA men also attended St. Patrick's College, but few mentioned it as a hotbed of Irish rebellion in their recollections of the revolutionary years. James Cahill, later a subordinate of Galligan's in the Cavan IRA and later still, a formidable Volunteer in the Dublin IRA Active Service Unit, recalled that in 1915-16, 'Father Dolan, St Patrick's College, a very sincere and patriotic Irishman, kept a small group of students, four or five, and myself in touch with the nationalist movement'.[6]

Physical force nationalism was rarely experienced in the Cavan of Paul Galligan's youth. But Irish nationalism – the idea that Ireland was a distinct nation, conquered in the past by England but striving to be free from it – was deeply ingrained in the region. Galligan himself remembered that 'I often heard the old people in Carrigallen talk about the Fenians and the Fenian Rising'.[7]

The Fenians or Irish Republican Brotherhood, in whose history Paul Galligan would go on to play an important part, had been founded in Dublin in 1858 to achieve Irish independence, by force if necessary.

At the time of the failed Fenian rising of 1867, the IRB had been relatively weak in Cavan. The organisation at that time was mainly centred in urban working class areas – especially in Dublin. However, when in the 1870s, the IRB adopted land agitation – obtaining security of tenure for tenant farmers and resisting evictions, alongside the goal of an Irish republic, they took off in the south Ulster and north Connacht area. By 1878, Cavan was behind only neighbouring Monaghan and slightly ahead of Sligo, Roscommon, and Leitrim as one of the strongholds of Fenianism.[8]

Paul Galligan's mother Sarah had been secretary of the Land League in Carrigallen.[9] The struggles of the Land War – the agitation for tenants' rights and ultimately ownership of land in 1870s and 1880s – had left their mark on people's political attitudes in rural Cavan. The Royal Irish Constabulary, or RIC, for instance, was widely unpopular for their role in trying to put down the land agitation. One Cavan IRA veteran, Seán Sheridan, remembered: 'There always had been a void between the people and the RIC. . . . The people had never forgotten the actions of the RIC during the Land League days and the Fenian rebellion and looked on them more as instruments of a foreign power than as a police force.'[10]

Fenianism in Cavan had faded somewhat in the following decades, as the Irish Parliamentary Party (or IPP) – dedicated to constitutional pursuit of Home Rule, or autonomy within the United Kingdom for Ireland – gained in popularity. Cavan had the highest per capita membership of the United Irish League in the country and also popular was the Catholic fraternal organisation, the Ancient Order of Hibernians.[11]

The West Cavan constituency, where Paul Galligan was elected as an MP for Sinn Féin in 1918, had been represented at Westminster since 1904 by Vincent Kennedy of the IPP – who was returned, unopposed in 1904, 1906 and 1910.[12]

But the beliefs of the supporters of the Irish Parliamentary Party and the United Irish League differed from the Fenians only in the means of securing Irish independence, not in the end itself. Home Rule was not seen by most nationalists as a final solution. Both radicals and moderates wanted Irish self-determination, both believed that Ireland and Irish Catholics had suffered from centuries of injustice at the hands of England. Both also celebrated past instances of armed resistance to English rule. There was an annual commemoration in Cavan town, for instance, for Myles 'Slasher' O'Reilly – an Irish Catholic soldier who had fought in the area in the 1640s.[13]

Within the Galligan family, Paul's nationalism was not at all out of place. His father would write to him in prison in 1917: 'I hope and trust in God that the Government will see their way to release the prisoners . . . and solve the Irish problem. That is if it is ever to be solved. Dear knows it's time a start was made after centuries of trouble and suffering.'[14] Myles 'Slasher' O'Reilly was reputed to be a remote ancestor of theirs.

While most people in Cavan at the close of the nineteenth century and opening of the twentieth did not support armed revolution in Ireland, this was not because of an opposition to Irish independence but because violence was seen as unnecessary and impractical when Home Rule could be achieved by peaceful means. When circumstances changed in 1913-1921, the electorate there largely threw their support behind the separatist Sinn Féin party and its armed auxiliary in the Irish Volunteers.

Along with Paul Galligan, the area around what would become the Irish border also threw up several other prominent rebel leaders in the 1916-21 period – Seán McDermott from Leitrim, Eoin O'Duffy from Monaghan, Seán MacEoin from north Longford and Frank Aiken from south Armagh.

'The Faith of our Forefathers'

Alongside Irish nationalism, and closely linked to it in Paul Galligan's upbringing, was Catholicism. Peter Galligan was a deeply religious man. He performed annually the pilgrimage to the shrine of St Patrick at Lough Derg, an experience he described to his son as 'one of the happiest events of my whole life'. The pilgrims had to fast on bread and water for three days, 'and perform the holy stations in your bare feet over the sharp stones and rocks which abound in your journey over the stations.'[15]

Paul shared his father's piety. Later, in prison, he reported: 'I go to communion every Sunday and assist at Benediction every Sunday evening and like every true Irish heart in sorrow and trouble I turn to the Sacred Heart of Jesus and Mary, "Our Mother of Sorrows", without consolation which not even our own nearest and dearest can give . . . in return we receive the tranquil peace and sympathy which none in this world can give.'[16]

At a personal level, the Galligans' faith was a source of strength and optimism to them. Peter Galligan put this in a straightforward way to his imprisoned son in 1917, 'Cheer up old man, don't be down-hearted, God will pull you through'.[17] Paul was often to write of how his faith was the only thing that kept him from utter despair at low moments in prison.

During the struggle for independence, Terence MacSwiney, the Sinn Féin Mayor of Cork who died on hunger-strike, would famously write that 'it is not those who can inflict the most, but those who can suffer the most who will conquer'. There is a distinctly Catholic flavour to the republican idea of victory through personal sacrifice – one shared by Paul Galligan.

His father, for instance, wrote of the pilgrims at Lough Derg: 'From the thousands who performed this station year after year since the days of St. Patrick, not a murmur is heard. They go through the suffering to make reparation to God for their past sins.'[18] In a similar vein, Paul Galligan wrote to his brother from prison in 1917: 'Forgive them [the British] father, they know not what they do. And those words of Christ dying on the cross is the answer and brings to us Irish convicts the great lesson of perseverance and submission and thus by humiliation and self-sacrifice won his glorious triumph over his enemies.'[19]

Personal faith was one aspect of Catholicism shaping Paul Galligan. Another important aspect was the specifically Irish Catholic identity – the feeling that the Irish people in essence were also the Catholic people, who had been persecuted in the past but were now resurgent. Galligan wrote of his religion as 'our faith to which our forefathers held so assiduously to in the past and though the days were numerous and the hours dark, this simple gift brought them victorious'.[20]

Paul Galligan's combination of religion and nationalism was not at all unusual for the time and place, indeed most Irish Catholics held similar views. Nor was it sectarian in the sense of excluding Protestants from the Irish nation, but it may have been heightened by the fact that in Cavan, and even more so in the other Ulster counties immediately to the north, there was another community, Protestant and Unionist, which defined itself quite differently.

Ulster Protestants, by and large, were hostile to Home Rule and joined organisations such as the Orange Order and later the Ulster Volunteers to resist it. By the late nineteenth century, discrimination against Catholics in Ireland was much less than it had been in the past, but there was still a feeling that the British authorities and their armed forces favoured the 'Orangemen' over Catholic nationalists. Peter Galligan wrote to his son in July 1918: 'The Country is inundated with [Dublin] Castle proclamations [banning meetings] and yet it appears that the Orangemen are to be given a free hand to hold meetings on the 12th. While the Croppys [Catholics] have to lie down.'[21]

Dublin and the IRB

In 1907, a 19-year-old Paul Galligan left the hills of Cavan for Dublin. The north Irish midlands were not a prosperous region. In County Leitrim, not far from the Galligans' home in Drumnalaragh, a failure of the potato crop in 1907-1908 threatened famine – a danger only staved off by emergency British government food aid to 1,000 families.[22]

There is no indication that the Galligans suffered from this level of poverty but clearly Paul Galligan felt there was more opportunity for him in Dublin. In the Irish capital Paul Galligan secured work in the drapery business and became an apprentice at Henry Street Warehouse. The big city must have been a big change for him. Only 91,173 people lived in all of County Cavan, but in Dublin city, 304,802 people lived cramped together in approximately 20 square kilometres between the two canals.[23]

No doubt in his free time, outside work, Paul Galligan looked around for things to do and places to make new friends in his new home. The young country boy did not drink or smoke. He later wrote of 'my total abstinence from alcohol or tobacco', but was a keen sportsman. Shortly after coming to

Dublin, he joined Kickhams Gaelic Football Club. The Gaelic Athletic Association, or GAA, founded in 1884, had, since the 1890s, been heavily infiltrated by the IRB and banned members of the police or British Army from becoming members. The president of Kickhams, James 'Buller' Ryan, was a Fenian 'centre' or cell leader.

It is probable that Paul Galligan already held nationalist views of some sort by the time he came to Dublin and these were no doubt strengthened by discussions with like-minded team mates after games and at club events.

'Buller' Ryan probably kept his eye on young Galligan for some time. In 1910 or 1911 – Galligan could not remember the exact date – Ryan proposed that he join the Irish Republican Brotherhood. Galligan duly joined the Henry Joy McCracken Circle, of which Ryan was 'Centre', at 41 Parnell Square, a five minute walk from his workplace, after swearing the following oath:[24]

> *In the presence of God, I, Paul Galligan, do solemnly swear that I will do my utmost to establish the independence of Ireland, and that I will bear true allegiance to the Supreme Council of the Irish Republican Brotherhood and the Government of the Irish Republic and implicitly obey the constitution of the Irish Republican Brotherhood and all my superior officers and that I will preserve inviolable the secrets of the organisation.*

Back in the 1880s, the IRB had had up to 40,000 members, but by 1910 it was a much smaller organisation, with around 1,300 activists, organised into cells or 'circles', each with a leader or 'centre'.[25] Galligan's group had six other members when he joined. At the top of the IRB was the Supreme Council, which handed down orders to the centres.

The McCracken circle, named after the executed United Irish leader of the 1798 rebellion in Ulster, had weekly lectures, mainly focused on historical subjects, such as the republican leaders of 100 years before – Robert Emmet and Wolfe

Tone. The members paid a small weekly subscription to cover expenses. 'At this time,' Galligan later recalled, 'there were no drills or instructions in military subjects. . . . There were no arms at this time.'[26]

The Brotherhood, or 'the organisation', as its members called it, was in the midst of a reorganisation. The IRB had lapsed into something of a drinking club for old Fenians in the early years of the twentieth century but was revived as a militant force by the efforts of a small number of energetic activists. Starting from Belfast, Dennis McCullough (a Belfast Catholic) and Bulmer Hobson (a county Down Quaker) had reinvigorated the IRB. From 1909, the veteran Fenian Tom Clarke and his younger protégé Seán McDermott began pressing for an armed rebellion in the years ahead.

The McCracken Circle had visits from the IRB executive: Bulmer Hobson, Gus Murphy, P.T. Daly and Mr. Deakin, who 'gave us lectures on the work we were doing and what we were expected to do'.[27]

In November 1910, around the same time as Galligan joined the Brotherhood, the new IRB generation founded the newspaper *Irish Freedom* to spread their message to the Irish public. This message, which Galligan must have absorbed at his lectures in Parnell Square, was one of uncompromising hostility to the Union between Ireland and Britain.

'The issue,' the first edition of *Irish Freedom* told its readers, 'is Irish Independence. . . . We have been told to forget history, to become practical people like the Scots and the Welsh.' The compromises of the constitutional nationalists in the Irish Parliamentary Party, aimed at securing Home Rule within the United Kingdom, were 'rotten and immoral'. 'The Irish attitude to England is war yesterday, war today, war tomorrow. Peace after the final battle.'[28]

For the IRB, Ireland, which was governed by British-appointed officials – the Lord Lieutenant, the Chief Secretary and the Under-Secretary for Ireland – lived under a tyranny based on armed force. 'Our country is run by a set of insolent officials, to whom we are nothing but a lot of people to be exploited and kept in subjection. The executive power rests on armed force that preys on the people with batons if they have the gall to say they do not like it.'[29]

Repression of the small republican movement in these pre-First World War days was not fierce, but was real. *Irish Freedom* complained that the police confiscated copies of their newspaper when it was delivered to the provinces and that detectives of the Dublin Metropolitan Police's (DMP) G Division followed their members home. On one occasion, an IRB man died as a result of a baton charge by the DMP during a protest at the visit of King George to Dublin in 1911. 'Hugh Holohan, a victim of police brutality during and prior to the visit of his Britannic majesty.'[30]

The IRB also blamed the British connection for all of Ireland's ills – poor industrial growth, poverty and emigration. 'Our land might be a garden for 20 million people, they have made of it a cattle ranch, supporting one fifth of its rightful population.'[31]

To right this situation, Home Rule, which would have kept command of the Army and police, foreign relations and taxation under British control, was simply not enough for the IRB. Paul Galligan later argued: 'Home Rule in a nut shell means a continuation of the present rule, for under it we get nothing, England controls taxes, revenue, customs, post office, commerce, etc. We simply would be an Irish Parliament for gathering taxes. We tell her, gather her own taxes and pay for the gathering.'[32]

The republicans had no time for the Home Rulers of the Irish Parliamentary Party – often known as 'Redmondites' after their leader John Redmond – who Galligan called 'the old gang of selfish imperial crawlers', interested only in advancing their careers at the expense of Irish nationality.

Redmond argued that Home Rule would mean 'a new Union, based on mutual respect'. *Irish Freedom* insisted that, 'If England wants a union she must take her garrison out of our country.' Well before the Rising of 1916, the IRB argued that Irishmen must be prepared to fight for independence, 'a dozen rifles are worth more than a thousand resolutions',[33] but as yet they were in a very small minority.

A series of events starting in 1913 would change this and open the door to armed revolt. The Third Home Rule Bill – fruit of the Irish Parliamentary Party's alliance with the Liberal Party at Westminster – was brought before the British Parliament in 1912.

In Ireland, Unionists, mostly Protestant and concentrated in northeast Ulster, but led by a Dublin lawyer, Edward Carson, came out in furious opposition to even limited autonomy for Ireland. The 'Ulster Covenant' of 1912 saw almost 500,000 Unionist men and women sign an oath to resist Home Rule. In January 1913, a Unionist militia, the Ulster Volunteer Force, was formed. It was armed surreptitiously over the following year.

For the IRB, the blocking of Home Rule by illegal means was an opportunity to turn the frustrated nationalist public towards the goal of full independence. Galligan recalled: 'On the formation of the Ulster (Carson) Volunteers in the north, volunteers were called from different [IRB] centres to form a class for military training.' Paul Galligan attended these military training classes, where he received instruction in drill, arms drill and signalling.

In November 1913, Eoin MacNeill, a Gaelic League scholar and academic and also in the future, a fellow-prisoner of the British with Paul Galligan in Dartmoor prison, founded the Irish Volunteers – a nationalist militia formed to apply pressure for Home Rule. He wrote that the Volunteers would 'show the Tories that the alternative to Home Rule was a policy of repression and coercion beyond any they had experience of', and 'show the Ulster minority that nationalist Ireland could not be treated with contempt'.[34]

'On the formation of the Irish Volunteers in November 1913,' Galligan recalled, he and his comrades in the IRB, 'were instructed to immediately join and take control.'[35] He may not have known it at the time, but Paul Galligan had taken the first steps on the road to revolution.

Endnotes

1. Colm Galligan, notes on Paul Galligan.

2. National Census Archive 1901, http://www.census.nationalarchives.ie/pages/1901/Cavan/Derrin/Drumnalaragh/

3. Paul Galligan to Monsignor Eugene Galligan, 4 May 1917.

4. Paul Galligan to Monsignor Eugene Galligan, 16 September, 1916.

5. Witness Statement of Peter Paul Galligan, Bureau of Military History (hereafter BMH) WS 170, file s2568.

6. Witness statement of James Cahill, WS 503, BMH, s.1760.

7. Galligan Witness statement BMH.

8. Tom Garvin, *The Evolution of Irish Nationalist Politics*, pp. 69, 72.

9. Galligan Witness Statement BMH.

10. Witness Statement of Seán Sheridan, BMH 1613, s2894.

11. Fearghal McGarry, *Eoin O'Duffy: A Self-Made Hero*, p. 3.

12. Brian M. Walker, ed. (1978). *Parliamentary Election Results in Ireland 1801–1922*. Dublin: Royal Irish Academy. pp. 164, 332-333.

13. Seamus McKenna Witness Statement BMH.

14. Peter Galligan to Paul Galligan, 6 June 1917.

15. Peter to Paul Galligan, 17 June 1917.

16. Paul Galligan to Eugene Galligan, 26 September, 1916.

17. Peter to Paul Galligan, 17 June 1917.

18. Ibid.

19. Paul to Eugene Galligan, 17 April, 1917.

20. Paul to Eugene Galligan, 26 September, 1916.

21. Peter to Paul Galligan, 6 June 1917.

22. Gerard MacAtasney and Seán MacDiarmada, *The Mind of a Revolution*, Drumlin 2004, p. 35.

23. 1911 Census.

24. Paul Galligan Witness Statement, BMH.

25. Gabriel Doherty and Dermot Keogh, *1916 – The Long Revolution*, pp. 103-108.

[26.] Galligan Witness Statement, BMH.

[27.] Galligan Witness Statement.

[28.] *Irish Freedom*, November 1910.

[29.] *Irish Freedom*, October 1911.

[30.] *Irish Freedom*, August 1911.

[31.] *Irish Freedom*, October 1911.

[32.] Paul to Eugene Galligan, 7 April, 1920.

[33.] *Irish Freedom*, June 1914.

[34.] Charles Townsend, *Easter 1916 – The Irish Rebellion*, pp. 52-53.

[35.] Galligan Witness Statement, BMH.

Chapter 2

1913-1916 – The Road to Rebellion

The Irish Volunteers was not an IRB front, it contained many nationalists who had previously been involved with organisations like the political party Sinn Féin and the cultural organisation, the Gaelic League. Officially, the Volunteers had been formed to make sure that Home Rule was passed. But to the IRB Supreme Council it was an unprecedented opportunity to mobilise nationalist Irishmen in arms and advance the goal of full independence.

Activists like Paul Galligan who already had experience of military training enabled the IRB to control the Volunteers. Galligan recalled: 'Our [IRB] class was distributed over the different units in the city area. I joined at Blackhall Place and we joined other units at the same time. . . . Our instructors were ex-British Army men and they were doing the drilling and organisation, but our men of the IRB were really in charge.'[1]

They had, as yet no military-grade rifles but small-calibre .22 rifles. Firing practice took place at the range in Clontarf, north Dublin. Galligan's sporting ties also helped in recruiting for the new movement – his Gaelic football club, Kickhams, formed a whole company and allowed their hall to be used for drilling.[2]

By June 1914, when the Volunteers took part in the annual rally at the grave of the 1798 United Irish leader Wolfe Tone in Bodenstown, County Kildare, Galligan recalled, 'it was noticeable that the IRB were well in control of the Volunteers now'. His IRB centre, Tom Hunter, was also the commander of the Volunteers' Second Battalion.

For many nationalists the Volunteers were simply a response to the Ulster Volunteers, a Catholic, nationalist reaction to Protestant, unionist aggression. But the IRB saw the situation not in terms of unionist against nationalist, or Catholic against Protestant, but in terms of Ireland against England.

The Volunteers, for the IRB, were to be the nucleus of an Irish Army that would demand independence. More than that, the IRB saw the movement as source of a new, confident Ireland that would not 'grovel at the feet of England' as the old Parliamentary Party did. 'The young men who stand together . . . for Gaelic League and Sinn Féin and Republican principles, who are crowding into the Volunteers, can save Ireland and will.'[3]

Nationalist discontent deepened in April 1914, when officers in the British Army base at the Curragh refused to move north and occupy positions against the threat of the Ulster Volunteers. An even greater provocation came in May, when the Ulster Volunteer Force imported some 50,000 rifles into Larne, without police or military opposition. By the summer of 1914, the numbers of young Irish nationalists 'crowding into the Volunteers' had reached 180,000.[4]

The Volunteers were now a serious enough force for both the British and the constitutional nationalists of the Irish Parliamentary Party to be concerned. In June 1914, John Redmond announced that the Parliamentary Party supported the Volunteer movement and after talks with Eoin MacNeill and Bulmer Hobson, he and other IPP leaders were co-opted onto the Volunteer Executive – much to the anger of the more hardline IRB figures like Tom Clarke and Seán McDermott.

Howth

If they were to be credible as an army, the Irish Volunteers needed weapons. Paul Galligan's battalion was mobilised for a route march to the fishing village of Howth, north County

Dublin, on 26 July, 1914. 'Through my IRB contacts, I knew there was something serious on, but did not know exactly what it was.'[5] In fact, they were to march to Howth harbour, to unload from the yacht the *Asgard*, a cargo of 900 rifles and 30,000 rounds of ammunition that Bulmer Hobson, the IRB leader, had secretly purchased in Germany.

Along the way, the Fianna, the youth wing of the Volunteers, brought up handcarts full of oak batons, 'which were handed out to selected men', including Galligan. At the quay in Howth, Galligan 'saw a yacht coming into the harbour. She hove-to at a point in the pier and made fast and the crew started handing out rifles to the Volunteers.'[6]

Before this the IRB and Volunteers had been mocked as 'playing at soldiers'. Paul Galligan must have felt exhilarated as he watched the rifles being brought ashore. Another participant, a Cumman na mBan (women's movement) activist, remembered that, at the sight of the arms being taken off the *Asgard*, 'we cheered and cheered and cheered and waved anything that we had and cheered again'.[7]

Galligan saw the coastguard fire off rockets to warn the authorities, but by that time all the rifles had already been handed out and the battalion was ready to march back to the city.[8] Galligan did not know it, but the commissioner of the Dublin Metropolitan Police, upon hearing of the arms landing, ordered the police, backed by British troops, to intercept the Volunteers, declaring that 'a body of more than 1,000 men armed with rifles marching on Dublin constitutes an unlawful assembly of a most audacious character'.[9]

Along the Howth Road, on the way back into the city, Galligan's battalion saw that 'British soldiers (Scottish Borderers) were drawn up across the road with bayonets fixed'. The soldiers had been ordered to seize the Volunteers' arms – though possession of weapons was not illegal in Ireland at the time.

The two groups of armed men came to a nervous halt close to each other and a Volunteer, Captain Judge, went to talk to the British troops. A melee broke out. One Volunteer named Burke who went to Judge's aid was stabbed with a bayonet in the knee. In the confusion, Paul Galligan and the other Volunteers were ordered to disperse and take their rifles with them. They slipped away through the north Dublin suburbs. Galligan and his club-mates of Kickhams football club made their way to their club house and left the rifles there.[10]

The day, which became known as the Howth gun-running, was a triumph for the Volunteers and a humiliation for the authorities. The British had not opposed the landing of Unionist arms at Larne but had now attempted to halt forcibly nationalists doing the same thing. Worse, from the British point of view, they had not succeeded in preventing the importation of the German Mauser rifles.

And even worse was to come for the British. The Scottish Borderers, who had failed in their mission to disarm the Volunteers, returned to the city to be jeered and stoned by a hostile nationalist crowd as they were marching back to Richmond Barracks along the Dublin quays. The troops opened fire on the taunting crowd on Bachelor's Walk, killing three bystanders and injuring 37.

Irish Freedom exulted: 'The Volunteer Movement has been formally baptised in blood. Proudly and in broad daylight the armed nation has been upheld. The young men are ready to fight for Ireland. Ultimate victory is very close now.'[11] The following week Paul Galligan's battalion held an exercise, armed, in the Dublin mountains.

The First World War and the Split in the Volunteers

Irish Freedom was exaggerating when it wrote of the 'final victory', but events certainly seemed to be going the separatists' way. The nationalist public had been provoked and angered by the blocking of Home Rule by the Ulster Volunteers. A nationalist militia, the Volunteers, partly under IRB control, was now armed and apparently heading for a confrontation with the police and military. But August 1914 saw a serious split in the Volunteer movement.

In August 1914, just as it looked as if the stand-off in Ireland between the Ulster and Irish Volunteers over Home Rule might develop into civil war, the conflict we now know as the First World War broke out. John Redmond pledged his Party's and the Volunteers' support to the British war effort. His thinking was that by proving nationalist loyalty to the United Kingdom, Home Rule would be more likely to pass. In fact, although Home Rule was passed in the British Parliament, it was postponed for the duration of the war and, as things turned out, never enacted.

On the ground, Redmond's support for Britain in the war split the Volunteer movement wide open. Those in the IRB and also other 'advanced' nationalists like Eoin MacNeill, who had formed the Volunteers, furiously rejected the idea that the Volunteers might join the British Army for the duration of the war.

The Volunteers divided into two antagonistic groups. On one side was the original Irish Volunteers, led by MacNeill, who refused to support the British war effort. They resolved to keep their organisation in Ireland and intact until Home Rule was passed. On the other side were the 'Irish National Volunteers', who followed Redmond and many of whom went on to join the British Army. By British estimates, 13,500 men stayed with the original Irish Volunteers, while Redmond took over 140,000 into the National Volunteers.[12]

In Paul Galligan's Dublin Brigade 'all companies . . . were ordered to parade and a notice was read which asked all Volunteers who were prepared to stand by the executive of the Volunteers to take a pace forward. Most of the men took a pace forward. Many of those who did not [take a step forward, thus showing their support for Redmond] did not take any further part in Volunteer activities after this. The Redmond or National Volunteers were now formed as a distinct organisation. . . . We lost a large amount of rifles and equipment owing to these defections.'[13] 'Redmond,' Galligan later remarked, 'had tried to break the movement.'[14]

The initial Irish nationalist support for the British war effort in Europe was a major blow to the radicals in the IRB. Paul Galligan wrote little about the world war in his letters, but no doubt he agreed with Seán McDermott, his fellow IRB man, who told a crowd in Tipperary in 1914: 'The Volunteers were not brought into existence to fight for England. To hell with England! Let her fight her own battles. The Volunteers are only intended to fight for Ireland!'[15] *Irish Freedom* pledged, 'Hatred to the Empire and Remember Bachelor's Walk!'[16]

On Redmond's urging, up to 200,000 Irishmen, among them 24,000 former Irish Volunteers, joined the British forces in the First World War and some 30,000 would die in it.[17] Redmond argued that the war was to 'defend the rights of small nations', like Belgium. But for IRB activists such as Paul Galligan, who saw in Ireland a small nation, oppressed by British imperialism, this argument carried little weight. Writing after the death of the Volunteer leader Thomas Ashe through force feeding on hunger strike in 1917, he argued that 'the death of Ashe has laid before the nations of the world what England is and how sincere her sympathy for small nations'.[18]

But whereas the IRB position was that those who joined the British Army were 'dupes and traitors',[19] Galligan privately acknowledged that many sincere Irish nationalists ended up fighting and dying in the war. Telling his brother Eugene of the death of a mutual friend from Cavan in the war, he wrote: 'I suppose you heard about Stephen Clarke being killed at the front, poor fellow. It was not his love of England that brought him out, for he was a staunch SF [Sinn Féiner], may the Lord rest his soul.'[20]

Aside from solely nationalist objections to Irish involvement in the war, though, Galligan, a strict Catholic, also disapproved of the social disruption caused by the demands of total war. Particularly objectionable to him was the idea of sending young women to the front as nurses or kitchen staff.

'What do we see – girls from the age of 16-25 taken away from all home restrictions, supervision or influence and transferred to camps and kitchens where . . . they will come in contact with millions of soldiers. Even in Catholic Ireland where Christian ideals has [sic] so long fought against this rottenness, we find since the war has started that this putrid war has at last broken down the barriers and touched our sainted land.

All I say is that God and Mary guard and protect any Irish Catholic girl whose patriotism may inspire [her] to join.'[21]

The Road to Insurrection

The Easter Rising of 1916 may not have happened had it not been for the outbreak of the First World War. The war gave those who wanted rebellion access to German arms and aid. It also distracted British attention from Ireland. 'England's Difficulty,' the old Fenian saying went, 'is Ireland's opportunity.' But there was also an element of desperation about the resort to force. The separatists were shocked and dismayed by the large-scale recruitment of nationalists to the British forces. Desmond Fitzgerald, a Gaelic League, Sinn Féin and IRB activist, later wrote: 'The reaction of the Irish people after the declaration of war filled me with the conviction that we had reached a point where the Irish people had accepted completely their absorption by the British.' If that happened, 'it would be futile to talk of ourselves other than as inhabitants of that part of England that used to be called Ireland. In that state of mind I had decided that extreme action must be taken.'[22]

Similarly, Paul Galligan wrote to his brother after the Rising, 'we were surrendering the last shred of Irish nationality and we knew that we had to fight to keep Ireland from becoming a British province'.[23]

There were, however, within the Volunteer leadership, two distinct schools of thought on the use of armed action. One, the position held by Eoin MacNeill and Bulmer Hobson, was that the Volunteers should not fight unless the British tried to ban their organisation, take their weapons and arrest their activists. If this happened, the Volunteers would fight in self-defence. Hobson, head of the IRB, in support of this argument, cited the organisation's constitution of 1879, which stated that the IRB would not launch another rebellion until it had the support of the majority of the Irish people.[24]

The other tendency, led initially by Tom Clarke and Seán McDermott, favoured launching a Rising regardless of what the British did. In May 1915, Clarke and McDermott, as well as like-minded Volunteer officers, Patrick Pearse, Thomas Mac-Donagh, Eamon Ceannt and Joseph Mary Plunkett, formed a secret 'military committee' to plan an uprising. In 1915, James Connolly, leader of the socialist republican group the Irish Citizen Army was also co-opted onto the committee. Clarke and McDermott represented the veteran Fenians, the others were sworn into the IRB after the outbreak of war.[25]

MacNeill and Hobson were not informed of the plans of the military committee for a rising until the very last minute and MacNeill, who believed it had no chance of success, would try to call the rebellion off.

Paul Galligan, who through his IRB contacts was rapidly rising through the Volunteers, was put on Thomas Mac-Donagh's staff in 1915. He may have known of the military committee's plans, but the details were known only to a handful of people and it seems unlikely that Galligan had more than a very general idea that something was going to happen before the war was over.

When explaining how the Rising had come about to his brother, Paul Galligan used a mixture of both the defensive arguments of MacNeill and the offensive ones of the military committee. On the one hand, he justified the Rising on the grounds that the British were about to suppress the Volunteers. 'As time went on the government and their spies, the "G" men [DMP detectives] were making things hot and we knew the hour was coming when we would have to either surrender our arms or fight for them.'

On the other hand, he also acknowledged that the Rising was a bid for independence. 'We knew it was Ireland's last chance but we were to wait till an hour when the Government was in a fierce struggle with Germany and when she would either have to withdraw troops to Ireland or give us all we demanded.'[26]

Was the suppression of the Volunteers really imminent in 1916? There was in fact fierce debate on this point within the British administration. Augustine Birrell, the Chief Secretary and Matthew Nathan, the Under Secretary were of the opinion that clamping down on the radical nationalist groups would be more politically costly than it was worth and would antagonise the nationalist community. On the other hand, Lord Lieutenant Wimborne and the British military intelligence argued insistently that 'seditious' groups must be disarmed.

Under the wartime Defence of the Realm Act (DORA), the British state in Ireland had extensive repressive legislation, but before the Rising, this was only irregularly used. *Irish Freedom* was closed down and its printing press seized in December 1914, as was that of *The Irish Worker*, James Connolly's newspaper. A number of IRB activists, notably Ernest Blythe, were arrested and deported for anti-recruitment agitation. Seán McDermott was given four months hard labour for a 'seditious' speech in Tuam, County Galway in early 1915. On the whole though, the Irish Volunteers were largely left alone in the months before the Rising.[27]

Galligan wrote that an armed parade on St. Patrick's day 1916 by the Volunteers in Dublin opened the eyes of the administration to the threat of a rebellion and that just before the Rising: 'The Privy Council met in the Lord Lieut. House in the [Phoenix] Park and it was there they decided to get 300 of the officers of the Volunteers arrested. A meeting of the Military Council of the Volunteers was called and it was decided to fight for this reason, that Monday would see all the Volunteer officers arrested and a general lifting of arms take place. . . . From Easter Sunday it was race between us and the Government but we got there first, even if it was only with a small force.'[28]

This was the argument used by the military committee to Eoin MacNeill, when the plans for the rebellion were revealed to him the day before the planned uprising. It was based on a Dublin Castle document leaked by a sympathetic civil servant to Dublin Corporation Alderman Tom Kelly, the week before the rebellion, which revealed a plan by the British military to arrest the leaders of Sinn Féin, the Irish Volunteers, the National Volunteers and the Gaelic League. Citizens of Dublin were to be confined to their houses and the city streets patrolled by troops. Patrick Pearse's school at St. Enda's was to be surrounded, as was MacNeill's house and that of the Catholic Archbishop of Dublin.

The British administration denied utterly the authenticity of the document and the British Army later asserted that it was merely a contingency plan to be used if conscription was imposed on Ireland. However Seán McDermott, just before his execution, swore to the priest who gave him absolution that the document was genuine and there is no doubt that the rebels themselves – including Paul Galligan – believed it.[29]

On the other hand, it also seems clear that the military committee had set a date for a Rising at some time in 1916. Seamus Doyle, a Volunteer and IRB officer from Enniscorthy, recalled that in late 1915, 'I was aware through IRB circles at this time that a Rising was planned, but I had no idea when it would take place'. In March of 1916, he met Patrick Pearse at the Emmet commemoration in Wexford and Pearse told him that 'the Insurrection was near at hand'.[30]

'Defiance to England'

Whether the action was to be offensive or defensive was a debate known to only a very small number at the top of the Volunteers and the IRB. For the rank and file Volunteers, their duty as they saw it was to remain in a state of readiness and by public display of arms and parades, show that not all Irishmen accepted Redmond's commitment to the British war effort.

Shortly after the Howth Gun Running and the split in the Volunteers, Paul Galligan was appointed Captain of G Company of the Dublin Brigade, which had its headquarters in the Iron Hall, Glasnevin. This small Company – reduced after the split with the Redmondites to 25-30 men – trained in the Hall and in Fairview where they held rifle practice. The officer of the company was Dick McKee, who in 1920 was shot by his British captors in Dublin Castle on the night of 'Bloody Sunday'.

The Company was armed with Howth Mausers, Lee Enfield rifles and revolvers. The Mausers imported at Howth were old models from the 1870s, which had to be reloaded after every shot, but which fired a heavy 11 millimetre bullet and, due to their long barrels, were highly accurate. The British Lee-Enfield, issued in 1907, was much superior – carrying a ten round magazine which could be fired at a rate of 15 rounds per minute. Galligan recalled, 'they had to be bought or got from British soldiers who carried their rifles with them on leave'.[31] The Volunteers depended heavily on the commitment of their members. All Volunteers of G/Coy had to pay personally for the rifles, which, Galligan remembered, left them with little spare money.

Initially the Irish Volunteers (nicknamed, inaccurately, after the split, the 'Sinn Féin Volunteers') were unpopular for their anti-war, 'pro-German' stance, while so many Irishmen were serving in the British forces. The *Irish Independent*, for instance, which was owned by William Martin Murphy, a former IPP MP, was openly hostile to the separatists. After the Rising, Murphy himself said 'that the authorities allowed a body of lawless and riotous men to be drilled and armed and to provide themselves with an arsenal of weapons and explosives was one of the most amazing things that could happen in any civilised country outside of Mexico'.[32]

Paul Galligan later wrote of the *Independent*, which he called 'Will Martin's dreadful', 'we are branded cut throats – renegades – anti-Catholic, anti-clerical and the usual scurrilous names by which we are known in the Irish press. But names do not harm, we smile on.'[33] Galligan, a deeply religious man, was clearly bothered by the allegation that the separatists and the IRB in particular were anti-clerical. The Fenians had indeed, since the 1860s, been condemned by the Catholic Church hierarchy, who backed the constitutional nationalists. But it is a mistake to see the Irish separatists as anti-clerical in the same way as, for instance, the contemporary republicans in France, who forcibly closed down Catholic run schools to enforce the separation between church and state.

Rather, the IRB, most of whom were practicing Catholics, insisted on the right to put the struggle for national independence before the dictates of the Church. Local priests often supported them. A Wexford IRB man, for instance, remembered attending a meeting at 41 Parnell Square (that Paul Galligan most likely also attended, it being the regular meeting place for his circle) where a Father Sheehy told the republicans that 'the IRB oath was not contrary to the teachings of the Church'. 'When we returned to Wexford we explained the position to our members and they all appeared to be satisfied.'[34]

In the summer of 1915, Paul Galligan was transferred to Thomas MacDonagh's staff as a staff officer. MacDonagh, who was an English Literature lecturer in University College,[35] was Director of Training of the Volunteers and also a member of the secret military council.

In August 1915, the Volunteers, along with the Citizen Army and representatives from Sinn Féin, the GAA and even the Redmondite National Volunteers, staged a show of strength at the funeral of Jeremiah O'Donovan Rossa – a veteran Fenian, who had led a bombing campaign in England in the 1880s.

On the day of the funeral, MacDonagh established his headquarters in a cab on Grattan Bridge, on the river Liffey. Paul Galligan's orders were to keep a clear passage from Grattan Bridge to City Hall for the Volunteers marching from the city centre to Glasnevin cemetery. A company of Volunteers were put at his disposal to keep the street clear.

'A superintendent of the DMP approached me in a furious temper,' Galligan recalled. 'He wanted to know under what authority I had stopped the thoroughfare. I informed him I was acting on the orders of my commanding officer. He said he did not recognise my commanding officer.'

The Superintendent accompanied Galligan to see MacDonagh and after a short argument, MacDonagh ordered Galligan to put the policeman under arrest. The Volunteers, it must be remembered, were armed and the Dublin Metropolitan Police were not, so there was little the Superintendant could do about his arrest. The humiliated policeman was detained until after the funeral. There could hardly have been a better symbolic turning of the tables on those who held power in Ireland.

The superintendent was still in Galligan's custody when the main body of Volunteers marched past in their dark green uniforms, wearing their distinctive Boer-style wide-brimmed hats and carrying rifles and bandoliers of ammunition. When the funeral procession passed, Galligan's Volunteers formed part of the rear guard and the column proceeded to Glasnevin. Commanding the rear guard was a Volunteer officer named Éamon de Valera – a man who would go on to play an important part in Paul Galligan's life.[36]

Being towards the rear of the procession, Galligan probably did not hear Patrick Pearse's graveside oration: 'The Defenders of the Realm have worked well in secrecy and in the open. They think that they have pacified half of us and intimidated the other half . . . but the fools, the fools, the fools! They have left us our Fenian dead and while Ireland holds these graves, Ireland unfree shall never be at peace.' Not many people actually heard Pearse on the day itself, but the oration later became a classic summing up of the Republicans' defiant attitude to British rule.

What Paul Galligan must have heard and what impressed a great many onlookers was the volley of rifle shots that crashed out over the grave when Pearse had finished speaking. A watching priest, Father Curran, thought, 'it was more than a farewell to an old Fenian. It was a defiance to England by a new generation in Ireland.'[37]

It must have been a tremendously exciting time for the 27-year-old Paul Galligan, who in his daily life still worked in a drapery warehouse on Henry Street. He was part of a movement that was openly parading armed in the streets of Dublin and defying the most powerful empire in the world. The episode with the policeman clearly stuck in his mind, as he still remembered it with clarity over thirty years later when giving evidence to the Bureau of Military History. If enough people refused to accept the authority of the institutions of the state, as he had done on Grattan Bridge that day, the British state would have to use force, or the foundations of British rule in Ireland would simply crumble into dust.

In September 1915, Paul Galligan attended a two-week training camp near Athlone. Apart simply from military training, this a chance to meet and get to know the Volunteer leaders from around the country. At the camp at Athlone were many men who would go on to play a central part in the independence struggle and, for those who survived, the formation of the Irish state: Terence MacSwiney, Austin Stack, Desmond Fitzgerald and Richard Mulcahy. J.J. 'Ginger' O'Connell was the officer in charge of the camp.

Another such occasion where Galligan, as Captain of G Company, mixed with the highest ranks of the Volunteers was at the Volunteer convention of October 1915. There, at the Abbey Theatre in Dublin, Galligan heard Michael O'Rahilly stress the need for intensified training and talk about the possibility of more arms being imported.[38]

Paul Galligan's whole life was not politics, drilling and arms training however. At some time in 1915 he became romantically involved with a young woman named Peg Hyland. Peg, who Galligan referred to rather stiffly in letters to his father as 'Miss Hyland', was 'a good religious girl' and 'we are very much attached to each other'. 'When I went down to Enniscorthy, I missed her a great deal.' He seems to have been worried that his father would not approve of the match, though, apparently due to Peg's humble origins, 'she may not be the sort of girl you would like me to choose but . . . after all Dad, money isn't everything'. Back in Dublin for the Christmas of 1915, the couple 'settled up things', and became engaged, although Galligan did not tell his father until his imprisonment in June 1916.[39]

Wexford

Paul Galligan found himself in Enniscorthy, separated from Peg Hyland, after he was posted there to help train the Enniscorthy Volunteers. A dispute had arisen in County Wexford between Brennan Whitmore, who was Officer-in-Charge of the Volunteers' Enniscorthy Battalion and the Brigade staff in Wexford. 'The dispute,' according to Galligan, 'was of a trivial nature and arose over the right of Volunteers to attend dances.' Brennan Whitmore wanted disciplinary action taken against men who spent their money on dances rather than on the arms fund. A rather unseemly squabble broke out and Whitmore ended up resigning. Thomas MacDonagh, the Volunteers' Director of Training, sent Paul Galligan down to the south-eastern town to sort out the mess and, as Galligan put it, 'to take charge of advanced training'.[40]

MacDonagh, as a member of the Military Council, knew that a Rising was looming and Enniscorthy was a very strategic military location, commanding the railway route to Dublin from the ports at Rosslare and Waterford. It was therefore important to get a reliable man in charge there who would carry out orders when the time came.

In Enniscorthy, Galligan, who was now known to the police and lived under the alias 'O'Reilly', was set up with a job in Bolger's drapery establishment.[41] In the evenings he intensively trained 26 local Volunteer officers, at their hall named 'Antwerp' in Enniscorthy. One Volunteer, John O'Reilly, remembered Galligan telling them, 'If the day would come, which we all believed was near, for a fight against the enemy (Britain), we would not have too many men and not enough officers.'[42]

The Enniscorthy Battalion, Galligan stated, 'was considered to be the finest unit in County Wexford'. One of the reasons for this was the strong IRB presence in the town and in the local Volunteers. One local IRB man, James Cullen, recalled the revitalisation of 'The Organisation' in the town after 1907, led by a man named Larry De Lacey. With the aid of old Fenians of the 1867 generation, one of whom, Charlie Farrell, was known to say, 'Ireland will never be free until Enniscorthy and every other Irish town runs red with blood', they recruited men carefully, selecting only those 'we knew held extreme national views'.[43] It may have helped their cause that they had the support of a local priest, Father Patrick Murphy, who according to his own testimony, 'was associated with Sinn Féin, the Volunteers and every National movement'.[44]

By 1913, there were over 100 sworn-in IRB members in the town and when the Volunteers were formed, they, like Galligan's circle in Dublin, joined and took over the organisation from the inside. They used their influence to keep Home Rulers and Hibernians away from positions of authority in the Volunteers and, for this reason, the local companies were not as affected as those elsewhere by the split over Redmond's support for Britain's war effort in 1914.[45]

There were also well organised companies in nearby Ferns and Gorey and others in Wexford town, Ballymurrin, Ballindaggin, New Ross along with a number of smaller units throughout the county. They were, however, very short of arms and ammunition.

Galligan's arrival in Wexford created a certain amount of confusion over who was in command of the Volunteers in the county. According to Seamus Doyle's Witness Statement, Seán Sinnott was appointed Officer Commanding of the Wexford Brigade and Paul Galligan was Vice Commandant.[46]

In Galligan's witness statement of 1948, he states that Seamus Doyle was the Officer in Charge.[47] However, in a letter in 1917 to his brother Eugene he states: 'I, as Senior Officer as well as by authority from Pearse took command and was responsible for all things in Enniscorthy till the order for surrender arrived on Sunday morning at 7.00 a.m.'[48]

According to Thomas Dwyer (Quartermaster, Wexford Brigade, Fianna Éireann), Seamus Rafter was the commanding officer. 'Enniscorthy stood in readiness for orders to start the Rising there, under the command of Commandant Seamus Rafter – a great leader and a great Irishman.'[49] John J. O'Reilly believed that Paul Galligan, Robert Brennan and Seamus Rafter were the senior officers in control, with Seamus Doyle as Adjutant.[50]

Even with hindsight, given the parallel workings of the IRB and the Volunteers in the rebels command structure and since orders were also coming from a secret military committee within the IRB, it is difficult to know who was really in charge. What is clear though, is that Paul Galligan's ties to the military committee, at the heart of the Rising, meant that he was the main source of accurate orders for County Wexford from the capital, once the Rising was underway.

In March 1916, Patrick Pearse visited Enniscorthy for the commemoration of Robert Emmet, the Republican leader hanged and beheaded for his rising of 1803. In public, in the Athenaeum theatre, Pearse delivered what Paul Galligan remembered as an 'impressive lecture' on Emmet and the Enniscorthy battalion provided a guard of honour. Such rallies, like the funeral of O'Donovan Rossa in Dublin, allowed the Volunteers to openly flout the authority of the British state. John O'Reilly remembered, 'we had the buildings under armed guard that night and were prepared to resist any interference from the RIC or other authorities'.[51]

In private, Pearse told senior local Volunteers such as Seamus Doyle and Paul Galligan, that the orders for an armed uprising would come soon. In the second week of April, the police seized a motor car in College Green, central Dublin, which contained a quantity of shot-guns, revolvers and ammunition, all of which were destined for County Wexford. The two occupants of the car were Irish Volunteers from Ferns.

The time for talking, drilling and marching was almost over. Paul Galligan had been a dedicated IRB activist for six years and an Irish Volunteer for three. Now, in late April 1916 he would be plunged into the chaos and danger of a real armed insurrection.

Endnotes

[1.] Galligan Witness Statement BMH.

[2.] Ibid.

[3.] *Irish Freedom*, March 1914.

[4.] Charles Townsend, Easter 1916 – The Irish Rebellion, p. 52

[5.] Galligan Witness Statement BMH.

[6.] Ibid.

[7.] Charles Townsend, *Easter 1916 – The Irish Rebellion*, p. 56

[8.] Incidentally, the coastguard who fired off the rocket was the maternal great-grandfather of Olga Ryan, Paul Galligan's future daughter-in-law.

[9.] Charles Townsend, *Easter 1916 – The Irish Rebellion*, p. 56.

[10.] Galligan Witness Statement BMH.

[11.] *Irish Freedom*, August 1914.

[12.] Charles Townsend, *Easter 1916 – The Irish Rebellion*, p. 68.

[13.] Galligan Witness Statement, BMH.

[14.] Paul Galligan to Monsignor Eugene Galligan, 29 November 1917.

[15.] Gerard MacAtasney and Seán MacDiarmada, *The Mind of a Revolution*, Drumlin 2004, p. 74.

[16.] *Irish Freedom*, October 1914.

[17.] David Fitzpatrick, 'Militarism in Ireland, 1900-1922', in Tom Bartlet, Keith Jeffreys, eds., *A Military History of Ireland*, p. 397.

[18.] Paul Galligan to Monsignor Eugene Galligan, 14 October, 1917.

[19.] *Irish Freedom*, March 1914 and October 1914.

[20.] Paul Galligan to Monsignor Eugene Galligan, 15 November 1917.

[21.] Paul Galligan to Monsignor Eugene Galligan, 6 March 1917.

[22.] Desmond Fitzgerald, *The Memoirs of Desmond Fitzgerald*, p. 80.

[23.] Paul Galligan to Monsignor Eugene Galligan, 29 November 1917.

[24.] Fearghal McGarry, *The Rising, Ireland Easter 1916*, pp. 98-99.

[25.] Charles Townsend, *Easter 1916 – The Irish Rebellion*, pp. 94-95.

[26.] Ibid.

[27.] Leon O Broin, *The Chief Secretary, Augustine Birrell and Ireland*, pp. 160-168.

[28.] Paul Galligan to Monsignor Eugene Galligan, 29 November 1917.

[29.] Charles Townsend, *Easter 1916 – The Irish Rebellion*, pp. 131-133.

[30.] Seamus Doyle Witness Statement, BMH.

[31.] Galligan Witness Statement, BMH.

[32.] Charles Townsend, *Easter 1916 – The Irish Rebellion*, p. 28

[33.] Paul to Eugene Galligan, 6 March and 6 April 1917.

[34.] James Cullen Witness Statement BMH.

35. Witness Statement by Mrs. Richard Mulcahy/Mary Josephine Mulcahy (Ryan) BMH.

36. Galligan Witness Statement, BMH.

37. Fearghal McGarry, *The Rising, Ireland Easter 1916*. p. 92.

38. Galligan Witness Statement, BMH.

39. Paul to Peter Galligan, 1 June 1916.

40. Galligan Witness Statement BMH.

41. Galligan Witness Statement BMH.

42. John O'Reilly Witness Statement BMH.

43. James Cullen Witness Statement, BMH.

44. Fr Patrick Murphy Witness Statement, BMH.

45. James Cullen Witness Statement, BMH.

46. Seamus Doyle Witness Statement, BMH.

47. Galligan Witness Statement, BMH.

48. Paul Galligan to Monsignor Eugene Galligan, 29 November 1917.

49. Thomas Dwyer Witness Statement, BMH.

50. John O'Reilly Witness Statement, BMH.

51. John O'Reilly Witness Statement, BMH.

Chapter 3

The Easter Rising

On the first day of the Easter Rising, Easter Monday, 24 April 1916, Paul Galligan made his way from the south Dublin suburb of Dalkey to O'Connell Street, central Dublin. The city's main thoroughfare had been occupied by armed men in dark green uniforms and slouch hats – the Irish Volunteers and Citizen Army.

Walking along O'Connell Street, Galligan stumbled upon a dead horse lying near Nelson's pillar – evidence of a skirmish between the Volunteers and a patrol of British cavalry – and noticed a tramcar that had been overturned and used to barricade the junction with North Earl Street.

Crowds of 'sightseers' milled around and some were looting some of the capital's finest shops in the northern end of the street.[1] Another onlooker on O'Connell Street, Ernie O'Malley, recorded that for those who lived in the slums off the street, 'this was a holiday. Some of the women . . . walked around in evening dress. Young girls wore long silk dresses. A saucy girl flipped a fan with a hand wristletted by a thick gold chain. . . . She strutted in larkish delight, calling to others less splendid, "How do yez like me now?".'[2]

Proceeding to the Tramway offices, where the rebels had established an outpost, Galligan was surprised to run into Brennan Whitmore, the Volunteer officer who had fallen out with the Enniscorthy battalion over the men going to dances.

Whitmore directed him to rebel headquarters at the General Post Office, or GPO. There, inside the grand Georgian building, Galligan assisted Volunteers to fortify the GPO against an expected British counter-attack. Later that night, Galligan met with three of the Rising's principal leaders, James Connolly, Patrick Pearse and Joseph Plunkett.

'Connolly said to me that they had enough men in Dublin and that it would be better to join my unit in Wexford. After a talk with Pearse and Plunkett in which I could hear the word "mountains" being used, Connolly instructed me to go back to Wexford as quickly as I could to mobilise the Enniscorthy Battalion and to hold the railway line to prevent troops coming through from Wexford as he expected they would be landed there. He said to reserve our ammunition and not to waste it attacking barracks or such like.'

It was now 2.00 am on Tuesday morning. Connolly told him to get something to eat – Desmond Fitzgerald gave him tea and two buns – and a 'good bicycle', which Gearoid O'Sullivan took from the GPO storehouse. At first light, 'I started straight away for Enniscorthy. It was just breaking day as I left the GPO. When I got to the Parnell monument, I looked back and I noticed that there were two flags flying from masts on the front of the GPO . . . a green flag and the tricolour of today.'[3] Paul Galligan's Easter Rising had begun.

'Carrying Out Orders'

The Easter Rising was a turning point not only in Paul Galligan's life but in Irish history. Before it, he had been heavily involved in the separatist movement, but he had yet to fire a shot in anger, be shot at or arrested. After Easter week, 1916, he would be in prison or openly engaged in a nationalist revolution for the next five years.

Similarly, before the Easter Rising, those demanding full independence from Britain had been a minority in Ireland. In the months and years after the Rising, not only did the majority swing behind the separatists, they would also vote for the actual establishment of an independent Irish Republic, in defiance of British law.

For such a pivotal event at both a personal and a national level, the remarkable thing about the Easter Rising is that it very nearly did not happen. Those who, like Galligan, were in the IRB knew that something was about to happen in the weeks leading up to the Rising, but the exact plans were known only to the handful of people – perhaps as few as seven – in the 'military committee'.

On Good Friday, 21 April, Seán McDermott and Patrick Pearse revealed the existence of the military committee and the plan for a Rising on Sunday to Eoin MacNeill, leader of the Volunteers. On the same day, orders were sent to the provincial leaders – in the case of Wexford, J.J. 'Ginger' O'Connell – to proceed with a Rising on Sunday. The Volunteer companies around the country were informed that they would parade with full kit on Easter Sunday, and to go to confession.

MacNeill, who had never been told of the preparations and who was against using force except in self-defence, was temporarily persuaded to go along with the rebellion on the grounds that the British were about to suppress the Volunteers and the nationalist movements generally and because it was revealed to him that a German ship, the *Aud*, was about to land with 10,000 rifles, ten machine guns and thousands of rounds of ammunition. Up to this, the Volunteers had at most 5,000 weapons in their possession in the whole country and many of these were obsolete.[4]

The *Aud* narrowly avoided several British patrol ships and convinced others that it was a Norwegian trawler. It anchored off Fenit in County Kerry for hours waiting for the local Volunteers to respond to their signals. In the meantime, it attracted the attention of British vessels in the area, who pursued it into Cork harbour. The *Aud's* captain sunk the vessel and its weaponry rather than surrender it. The following day a U-boat landed Roger Casement, the Volunteers' contact with Germany, nearby at Fenit. Before he could do anything, however, he was arrested by a suspicious policeman.[5] He would be hanged in August for treason.

MacNeill, now convinced that the Rising would be a bloody failure, tried to call it off. Taking out an advertisement in the *Sunday Independent*, he ordered: 'Owing to the very critical position, all orders given to Irish Volunteers for tomorrow, Easter Sunday, are hereby rescinded, and no parades, marches, or other movement of Irish Volunteers will take place. Each individual Volunteer will obey this order strictly in every particular.'

On Saturday evening, MacNeill had a lengthy meeting at 54 Rathgar Road, Dublin with a number of the leading Republicans, including Cathal Brugha, Seán T. O'Kelly and Thomas MacDonagh. At the end of the meeting, Mary Ryan was despatched to Wexford with the following note from MacNeill: 'There will be no manoeuvres tomorrow. All manoeuvres are cancelled. This is to be obeyed by every officer.' On Easter Sunday morning, Mary Ryan arrived in Enniscorthy and met with Ginger O'Connell, Seamus Doyle, Fr. Pat Murphy along with others and relayed the message.[6]

MacNeill, however, managed to postpone the Rising by only 24 hours. Those in the Military Committee, who were committed to rebellion, managed to get word to reliable units in Dublin that the Rising was going ahead and at noon on Monday, the 24th, over 1,000 Volunteers and Citizen Army fighters seized strongpoints all over Dublin city centre. In O'Connell Street, where Paul Galligan met James Connolly and the other leaders, they proclaimed an Irish Republic. Five days of bloody fighting in the capital would ensue in the coming week.

In the provinces, however, the stream of contradictory orders coming from Dublin caused chaos among the Volunteers. J.J. O'Connell, who was supposed to be in command of the Rising in the south-east, told Seamus Rafter, Seamus Doyle and Paul Galligan that 'he would take no part in the forthcoming rising and, further, it would be our responsibility whatever action we took'.[7]

The Volunteer officers in Enniscorthy were, understandably, at a loss. Galligan remembered: 'As a result of O'Connell's actions we were left without instructions and could take no further action and on Easter Saturday there was an air of indecision prevailing among the officers owing to this lack of instruction.'

It was for this reason that Paul Galligan had travelled to Dublin late on Easter Saturday night. On Sunday, he read MacNeill's order cancelling 'manoeuvres' and assumed that the Rising was off. But the following day, put up in a house in Dalkey, he learned of the events in the city centre and went to O'Connell Street to try to find out in person what was going on and what was expected of the Enniscorthy Volunteers.

Some of those who had planned the rebellion and those who had fought in it afterwards bitterly criticised MacNeill's actions, which they felt had sabotaged the chance of nationwide rebellion. Those in the IRB felt even more betrayed by Bulmer Hobson, head of that organisation, which supported MacNeill, and who as a result was kidnapped by armed IRB men and held for a week in house in the northside of Dublin. Some even talked of shooting him.[8]

Paul Galligan, however, wrote to his brother Eugene in 1917, 'let me say that MacNeill did what he thought was right and what I would have done was I in his position'.[9] When asked by Father Patrick Murphy during the Rising about the prospects for success, he replied, 'I told him that the arms ship had been sunk and that we were only carrying out our orders and I believed there was no hope of success'.[10]

Nevertheless, Galligan was more fortunate than many provincial Volunteer officers in that he had received clear and realistic orders from the head of what was now calling itself the Army of the Irish Republic – get back to Enniscorthy and cut the railway line to prevent the British from bringing reinforcements back to Dublin.

The Rising in Enniscorthy

Getting back to the south-eastern town was far from straight-forward, however. Connolly had told Galligan not to go back by Wicklow, the most direct route, since he believed it was blocked by British troops. Instead, Galligan took a wide detour, via the North Circular Road, Mulhuddart and Maynooth and through County Carlow – making the journey half as long again (around 200 kilometres) than the most direct route. At Maynooth, he saw troop trains proceeding towards the city, carrying some of the 16,000 troops the British would deploy to crush the insurrection in Dublin.

The postman's bicycle he was riding was described, by the standard of the day, as 'a good bicycle'. But it would have been a heavy, clunky machine, with only one gear. Paul Galligan's arms, legs, neck and backside must have ached unbearably as the hours went by on the back roads on which he cycled throughout Tuesday. 'I travelled all day and late that night I arrived at some place in County Carlow, the name of which I can't remember. I got a bed in a hotel there and stayed the night.' It was late on Wednesday evening before he reached Enniscorthy. On the outskirts of the town he happened across a Volunteer who was delivering bread and told him to gather the officers, because he had instructions for them from James Connolly.

In Enniscorthy itself, since Paul Galligan's departure for Dublin, the local Volunteers, under Seamus Doyle, had received an order from Pearse on Monday afternoon, telling them, 'we start at noon today, obey your orders'. Since it was not at all clear what these orders were, Doyle consulted with Sinnott, the Brigade commander in Wexford town, who told him, 'in consequence of the conflicting orders he would not have anything to do with the matter'. Back in Enniscorthy on the Tuesday, Doyle found a few Volunteers waiting at the ammunition dump, unsure of what to do.[11]

It was only Galligan's return with Connolly's orders that galvanised the Enniscorthy men. James Cullen recalled: 'A meeting of the officers was held and Commandant Galligan gave full details of the fighting in Dublin and of the positions held by the Volunteers. It was then decided to rise. It was really Commandant Galligan who was responsible for this decision.'[12]

At the conference on Wednesday night, they decided to take action the following morning. In the early hours of Thursday, around 100-200 Volunteers took over the town hall and the castle and surrounded the RIC barracks in the town, to which they cut off the supply of gas and water. The insurgents' armaments were meagre – just 20 rifles and 2,000 rounds of ammunition. Many carried only pikes, which, effective enough in 1798, would have been useless in an encounter with either armed police or British troops in 1916. The Enniscorthy Volunteers were very conscious of themselves as heirs of the 1798 rebels in County Wexford. One of the symbolic actions they undertook was to occupy Vinegar Hill, scene of the United Irishmen's final defeat in 1798, and from there fire some shots at the RIC barracks.

The Athenaeum theatre was made the Republicans' headquarters, over which they flew the green, white and orange tricolour. All the public houses in the town were closed down and as Father Patrick Murphy, a sympathetic priest, who publicly blessed the rebels, recalled, 'during the four days of Republican rule, not a single person was under the influence of drink'. The railway station was taken over and a train to Arklow was stopped and commandeered.[13]

Paul Galligan was officer in charge of field operations and commanded a guard of honour as the Republican flag was raised. Seamus Doyle issued the Proclamation of the Republic, 'calling on the people to support and defend it'.[14]

Whereas in Dublin the rebels were initially highly unpopular with the general public, in Enniscorthy the reaction to the Rising seems to have been largely positive. According to Seamus Doyle, 'feeling in the town was generally friendly towards us, excepting the families of some British Army soldiers.'[15]

Seán Etchingham of Gorey was in charge of recruiting and recruits. Not only did Volunteer companies come in from Gorey and Ferns, but hundreds of local men and boys wanted to join the rebels, Galligan recalled. 'Large numbers of men were presenting themselves to join us and our biggest problem was feeding these men.' Cumman na mBan, for whom Galligan felt 'nothing but admiration and appreciation is due', helped to house and feed the new arrivals.[16] Even two of the local priests – Fr. Coad and Fr. Murphy – were anxious to join the Enniscorthy Volunteers, but were persuaded otherwise and left after blessing the men.

Part of the reason for the Wexford rebels' popularity may have been that the rebellion in Enniscorthy was, in stark contrast to Dublin (where almost 500 people lost their lives), nearly bloodless. There was a brief exchange of shots between the Volunteers and the RIC, in which two civilians and an RIC constable were wounded, but the rebels never tried to assault the barracks; they had been ordered not to waste their limited ammunition by doing this.

Another factor was that the Volunteers made great efforts to present themselves as responsible soldiers and representatives of an Irish government. The prohibition on drunkenness was a reaction against allegations of drunken anarchy and looting in past Irish rebellions, above all in County Wexford itself in 1798. In 1916, according to Paul Galligan: 'All of the officers and most of the men were in uniform. . . . Food, bedding, cars (which were returned to the owners after the surrender) and clothing were commandeered from local shops and receipts were issued in all cases. It was admitted in all cases afterwards that there was no undue commandeering and no one was victimised on account of his political leaning. The police [RIC] in the town were put off-duty and confined to barracks. We established our own police and town patrols.'[17] In spite of this, owing mainly to the destruction of roads and rail lines, the estimated damage to property in the Enniscorthy Rising came to £3,000.[18]

Old grudges between the Home Rulers and the Republicans were not dredged up during the Rising in Enniscorthy – some National Volunteers and one Irish British soldier actually joined the rebels. But, as Volunteer James Cullen reported, there were limits to the Volunteers' magnanimity, 'nearly all the [British] loyalists were visited by Volunteers and arms and motor cars seized'.[19]

The diary of Seán Etchingham, a future Dáil government minister, conveys the sense of liberation and exhilaration the Volunteers experienced: 'We had at least one day of blissful freedom. We have had Enniscorthy under the laws of the Irish Republic for at least one day and it pleases me to learn that the citizens are appreciably surprised . . . a more orderly town could not be imagined. The people of the town are great. The manhood of Enniscorthy is worthy of its manhood.'[20]

The station at Enniscorthy was in their possession but an effort to blow up the railway bridge at Eddermine came to nothing. Two Volunteers who were in the process of laying the explosives were surprised and fired on by an RIC patrol, who captured them both.

By Saturday morning, up to 1,000 Volunteers had been mobilised. News had reached the Volunteers, via some railway workers, that the British garrison in Arklow was preparing an assault. Galligan decided to establish a strong outpost at Ferns, which would 'act as a buffer and take the first onslaught of the British army and provide time for the Enniscorthy Volunteers to deploy and prepare for an attack'. Galligan led 40-50 men to Ferns, where they took over the RIC barracks, which had been vacated by the police and the national school. Roads were blocked and advanced posts of scouts established. A telegraph discovered in Ferns barracks stated that 'enormous force would be required to suppress it [the rebellion]'.[21]

On Saturday, the RIC County Inspector reported: 'The rebels are concentrated at Enniscorthy and are stated to be entrenching themselves there, the Police are still holding out [presumably in the police barracks]. The approaches to Enniscorthy within a radius of three miles of the town were blocked with felled trees and in one case by a telegraph pole which had been brought down. The damage to the Barrow Bridge on the

Dublin and South Eastern Railway is now reported not to be serious.'[22]

Meanwhile, the British War Office sent a telegraph to Lieutenant-Colonel G.A. French, a retired British Army Officer who lived about two miles outside Wexford in Newbay, instructing him to take over the command of the British Forces in Wexford and advising that reinforcements were on their way from Waterford along with an armoured train with a field gun.

Patrick Pearse had in fact already surrendered on Friday afternoon on behalf of the Republican forces in Dublin, 'to prevent the further slaughter of the civilian population and in the hope of saving our followers, now hopelessly surrounded and outnumbered'.[23]

In Wexford, the British assembled a column under French of 1,000 men, two field guns and a 4.7 inch naval gun at Wexford town, 'with a view to engaging the rebels at Enniscorthy'.[24] The poorly armed Volunteers could not have taken on a force with this kind of firepower in a pitched battle. Perhaps fortunately for all concerned, they did not try to.

According to James O'Connor, a Home Ruler who joined the RIC as a Special Constable for the duration of the Rising, Colonel French sent word to a Protestant clergyman and Dr. Furlong, the administrator of the Catholic parish of Enniscorthy, suggesting that they should seek out the leaders of the Rebellion and advise them that they had no hope of victory and that there would be considerable loss of life and damage to property if he had to shell Enniscorthy. If they surrendered: 'All the leaders and the men would be allowed to walk out of town. Colonel French was a gentleman and kept his word. But what explanation he gave to the British War Office I do not know.'[25] However, while Seamus Doyle records meeting Furlong, his and the other Volunteers' accounts state that it was Pearse's surrender order, conveyed by the British to the Volunteer leaders in Wexford, that ended the Rising in Enniscorthy.

The Surrender

By Sunday morning, there had still not been any sight in Enniscorthy or Ferns of the British Arklow garrison or the mobile column from Cobh or Wexford. Later that afternoon, one of the Volunteers' cycle patrols returned to the outpost at Ferns and told Galligan that an RIC District Inspector and Sergeant had arrived under a flag of truce with a copy of Pearse's surrender order.

Galligan was sceptical and instructed the Volunteer to take the two policemen to the local hotel, where he interviewed them. He inspected Pearse's surrender order which was addressed to the O/C Enniscorthy Volunteers. Galligan sent them to Enniscorthy under armed escort which travelled in the second car. At the time of receiving the surrender, a British troop ship had arrived in Waterford and its troops were marching to Enniscorthy.[26]

At first, Seamus Doyle and his officers in Enniscorthy refused to believe the surrender order. He and Seán Etchingham of Gorey applied to Colonel French for permission to travel to Dublin and see Pearse in person. Despite the misgivings of the local RIC, who wanted the pair arrested, French put them in a military car and had them driven to Arbour Hill prison in Dublin where Pearse was being kept. Pearse looked 'physically exhausted but spiritually exulted. He told us that the Dublin Brigade had done splendidly – five days and nights of continuous fighting. . . . Etchingham said to him, "Why did you surrender?" Pearse answered, "because they were shooting women and children in the streets. I saw them myself."'[27]

This appears to be a reference to an incident Pearse witnessed on Friday 28 April, when three elderly civilians, trying to escape the fighting in Moore Street, advanced towards the British positions carrying white flags, but were cut down by machine gun fire. According to Seán McDermott, 'when Pearse saw that, we decided we must surrender to save the lives of the citizens'. Also that day, British troops had broken into houses on North King Street and killed 15 civilians whom they accused of being rebels, but Pearse had not seen and probably did not know about this.[28]

Pearse had not been aware of the Rising in Enniscorthy but agreed to sign a written order to the Wexford Volunteers confirming the surrender, which Doyle and Etchingham brought back to Enniscorthy.[29] Doyle and Etchingham returned to Enniscorthy on Monday, 30 April. Paul Galligan, still in Ferns, received a dispatch from Enniscorthy confirming the surrender order and telling him to return to the town. Still thinking of the need to behave as responsible soldiers, who respected the rights of property, Galligan, supervised a clean-up. 'I was anxious to see that everything in Ferns was left in the same condition as we found it.' So, while his men and their arms were ferried back to Enniscorthy in cars, he was one of the last to leave Ferns.

Some of the Volunteers in Enniscorthy, such as James Cullen, took to the hills in the hope of starting a campaign of guerrilla warfare, but after a few days decided to come back down and 'face the music'. Those who remained formally surrendered to Colonel French and were taken by ship to captivity in Dublin.[30] If French had indeed promised to let the rebels 'walk out of town', he was unable to deliver on his commitment.

It might have seemed, during the Republican occupation of Enniscorthy, that everyone in the town was on their side, but after the Rising 200 of the Volunteers' various political opponents in Enniscorthy, who had lain low during the rebellion, 'National Volunteers, Hibernians, and Unionists', helped the RIC to patrol the town. As one Republican, Máire Fitzgerald, bitterly recalled, 'the rats all came out of their holes to welcome the British soldiers'.[31] Volunteer John O'Reilly was shocked to see the British Army entering Enniscorthy, 'accompanied by some of the Wexford (so called) National Volunteers or Redmondites'.[32]

Enniscorthy was a particular stronghold of radical nationalism – the RIC noted that the Irish Volunteers, Sinn Féin, the Gaelic Athletic Association and the Gaelic League (and though they didn't know it, the IRB) were the most influential organisations there. Elsewhere in the county, the IPP, the Ancient Order of Hibernians and the National Volunteers were dominant and those places remained hostile to the rebellion.

The RIC Yearly Police report for 1916 writes of Wexford: 'Apart from the places affected by the rebellion, the county was peaceable during the year. . . . Elsewhere in the county, the feeling of the people was quite hostile to the rebels and large numbers assembled under arms to assist the police in the towns of Wexford, New Ross and Gorey.'[33]

Arrest

Paul Galligan had not surrendered, however. On his way back to Enniscorthy, his inexperienced Volunteer driver crashed their car into a ditch, badly injuring a Cumman na mBan girl, Peg Walsh, who was in the car. By the time Galligan got to Enniscorthy, the Volunteers had either dispersed or been arrested.

One of the Cumann na mBan girls, Chrissie Moran, informed Galligan, exhausted and dazed by the effects of the crash, that there was a vacant house belonging to her brother-in-law in the town and that Galligan and the driver could rest there. They entered by the back door. Later that day, Galligan was awoken by a knock on the door. The driver, who was in the kitchen at the time, came to Galligan and advised him that it was the military at the door: they were carrying out house-to-house searches. The people next door shouted to the military that there was no one there and the soldiers went off without searching the house. Later that evening, Chrissie Moran brought them food and civilian clothes and Galligan gave her his uniform.

The following day, travelling once again by bicycle, he started out on the long journey home to County Cavan. His remaining men hid their arms and went home.[34] The authorities were looking for Galligan. Wexford Volunteer John O'Reilly, who was arrested on 2 May 1916, recalled: 'It appeared that they had heard the name of a Captain O'Reilly, a very prominent officer. This was Paul Galligan . . . but they had the wrong name and they seemed to think that I was the man they want-ed. I refused to give any information, only that I was in En-niscorthy and I knew nothing about anybody.'[35] 'O'Reilly' was the pseudonym Galligan had been using since he was posted to Enniscorthy.

Galligan cycled to Cavan in manageable stages, via Carlow and Mullingar, sleeping in sympathisers' houses along the way. He arrived back in the family home at Drumnalaragh, 'on the Friday or Saturday after the surrender'. He was utterly spent by his efforts, 'the whole week of the rebellion I had not had a single hour's sleep'. On Monday, two weeks after he had spoken to James Connolly in the GPO in Dublin, the Galligan home was surrounded by armed RIC men and Paul Galligan was arrested. He did not resist.

John Maxwell, the British Commander in Chief, sent mo-bile columns of cavalry, infantry and armoured cars through-out the country to disarm the Volunteers and arrest nationalist suspects. A total of 3,430 men and 79 women were rounded up, though 1,400 were released within a week.[36] In County Wexford, 270 men were arrested after the rebellion, of whom ten were sentenced to imprisonment or penal servitude.[37]

Not all those arrested were hardened rebels. During John O'Reilly's detention, Matt Kerns of Ferns was brought in to the detention centre. An RIC officer dumped some of his belong-ings onto the floor, the contents of which included Irish kilts, badges, a Confraternity medal and ribbon. The head constable started to question Kerns, who looked very innocent. 'Are you a member of any secret society?' the constable asked. With great innocence in his voice, Kerns replied, 'Yes, the Confra-ternity of the Sacred Heart.'[38]

Death Sentence and Reprieve

Galligan was taken to Dublin, and after some nights in Ar-bour Hill prison and Kilmainham Gaol, he was housed with other internees in Richmond Barracks. His Witness Statement records, matter of factly: 'We slept on the floor. Sanitary ar-rangements were very bad. We were issued with a couple of blankets. Food was reasonable and we were allowed to write letters.'

Martial law had been declared and the rebels were tried by military court-martial. On 14 May 1916, Galligan was brought before a court of three military officers and was charged with 'being an officer in charge of armed rebellion which waged war against his Majesty the King at Enniscorthy'. An RIC sergeant testified that he had seen the accused at Ferns with a rifle and revolver. Galligan, still the defiant Irish rebel, replied 'that the charge was correct and that I was proud of having fought for my country and the only regret I had was that we had not succeeded'.[39]

After the hearing, Galligan was transferred from Richmond Barracks to Kilmainham Gaol and placed in a cell in the top wing. Some days later, Galligan was informed that he had been sentenced to death. He was then taken to one of the condemned cells beside the execution yard. While in the condemned cell, Father Sylvester from Church Street heard his confession.

In total over 90 rebels (including Eoin MacNeill, who had tried to call off the Rising) were to be executed on the orders of General Maxwell, in the aftermath of the rebellion. Fifteen were shot by the time the British government, concerned at the effects the shootings would have on Irish public opinion, intervened to halt the executions. On 21 May, Paul Galligan heard that his sentence had been commuted to five years' penal servitude.

Galligan was clearly, by this point, at the very limit of his physical and mental endurance. He wrote to his brother in 1917 when he heard that his sentence had been commuted: 'In fact I was sorry, for I was prepared for the death and it would have been a relief then as the whole week of the Rebellion I had not a single hour's sleep and when then on 21 May after sleeping for three weeks on cold floors and in your clothes without a change, death was preferable to another week of it.'[40]

By the time Galligan's sentence was reprieved, all the men who had planned and led the rebellion in Dublin (with the sole exception of Éamon de Valera) were dead. The leaders of the Rising were tried in secret and 15 shot between the 3 and 12 May. Pearse, Tom Clarke and Thomas MacDonagh were the first to be shot, only four days after their surrender. James Connolly, who was badly wounded, was the last. He had to be tied to a chair in order to face the firing squad.

In Kilmainham Gaol, Galligan heard grisly details of Connolly's death from an NCO. The executions, the soldier told him, took place with the executed men sitting on boxes. Because of Connolly's injuries, he was not handcuffed or tied and was shot sitting on a chair. Connolly grasped one of the rungs of the chair and, on being shot, he fell forward and the rung came away from the chair and remained in Connolly's hand. Galligan actually saw this chair without the rung in Kilmainham. One of the Dublin Fusiliers who escorted the Volunteers to Dartmoor Prison, told Galligan that he had been in Arbour Hill Prison when an ambulance brought in Connolly's body and Connolly was buried with the rung in his hand.[41]

Not long afterwards, Galligan and his fellow prisoners were taken across the Irish Sea to Dartmoor prison in the south-west of England. It must have seemed at the time like the end of all their hopes. As things turned out though, the prison experience proved to be an opportunity for the Republicans to launch a new phase of the struggle.

The Rising in Wexford – A Failure?

Nearly thirty years later, in the Dáil, the independent Irish parliament, Deputy Corish of Wexford complained that only 70 of the 260 men who had submitted claims for a state pension for their service in the Easter Rising in Enniscorthy had had their claims accepted. 'The Departments of Finance and Defence insist that the Enniscorthy men had no contact with the enemy. The Enniscorthy men came out to establish the Republic and were prepared to die for the Republic, if necessary. They came out under the order of Pearse and never thought that the struggle was going to end so quickly.'[42]

Without doubt, Paul Galligan and his comrades in Ferns and Enniscorthy were prepared to fight the British forces. They surrendered only with great reluctance when they received orders to this effect in person from Patrick Pearse.

The outcome of any battle in Wexford, however, was not in doubt. The poorly armed Volunteers might have made a good stand – only 17 Volunteers at Mount Street in Dublin had held off a regiment for two days and killed and wounded 240 British troops – but they would certainly have been beaten. Many of them and probably many civilians also, would have been killed had Enniscorthy been bombarded by the British heavy guns. Paul Galligan himself said during the week that without the German arms, they 'had no hope of success'.

So why rise at all? For one thing, Galligan had clear and achievable orders from James Connolly to block the railway line to Dublin. There was also a certain amount of personal pride at stake. Paul Galligan wrote to this brother that 'all the officers of Wexford decided to fight, even if it was only for 12 hours as they would not stand by and watch their brothers in Dublin fall without striking a blow'.[43]

As in Dublin, the Volunteers in Wexford showed they were serious about fighting and, if necessary, dying for an Irish Republic, a fact that greatly increased their prestige among the Irish nationalist public. Moreover, in the longer term, the British reaction to the Rising – wholesale arrests and executions – pushed many moderate nationalists, who had been hostile to the Rising, into the separatist camp.

In County Wexford, the RIC reported: 'Although the majority of people did not approve of the rebellion and were anxious that law and order should be maintained, they were unwilling to see any of the rebels punished and their punishment excited considerable sympathy.'[44]

The majority of Irish people had not been consulted about the rebellion and were shocked at the prospect of death and destruction that it brought, but they remained Irish nationalists and were unwilling to side with the British against their kith and kin. Within the next two years, this reaction against the British repression of the Rising would turn men like Paul Galligan from defeated and reviled prisoners into national heroes.

Endnotes

1. Galligan Witness Statement, BMH.

2. Ernie O'Malley, *On Another Man's Wound*, pp. 40-41.

3. Galligan Witness Statement BMH.

4. Charles Townsend, *Easter 1916 – The Irish Rebellion*, p. 143, British military Intelligence calculated they had 4,800 rifles, shotguns and revolvers in their possession, along with home-made grenades and bayonets.

5. T. Ryle Dwyer, *Tans Terror and Troubles Kerry's Real Fighting Story*, pp. 84-85.

6. Mary Ryan Mulcahy, Witness Statement, BMH.

7. Galligan Witness Statement, BMH.

8. Charles Townsend, *Easter 1916 – The Irish Rebellion*, p. 137.

9. Paul Galligan to Monsignor Eugene Galligan, 29 November 1917.

10. Galligan Witness Statement BMH.

11. Seamus Doyle Witness Statement, BMH.

12. James Cullen Witness Statement, BMH.

13. Father Patrick Murphy Witness Statement, BMH.

14. Seamus Doyle Witness Statement, BMH.

15. Seamus Doyle Witness Statement, BMH.

16. Galligan Witness Statement, BMH.

17. Ibid.

18. RIC Annual Report 1916, p. 11.

19. James Cullen Witness Statement, BMH.

20. Father Patrick Murphy Witness Statement, BMH.

21. Galligan Witness Statement, BMH.

22. Daily Police Reports, 1916 Rebellion, WO 35/69/1, The National Archives, Kew, Richmond, Surrey, TW9 4DU, England.

23. Charles Townsend, *Easter 1916 – The Irish Rebellion*, p. 246.

24. Daily Police Reports, 1916 Rebellion.

25. James O'Connor Witness Statement, BMH.

26. Galligan Witness Statement, BMH.

27. Seamus Doyle Witness Statement, BMH.

28. Charles Townsend, *Easter 1916 – The Irish Rebellion*, p. 246.

29. Seamus Doyle Witness Statement, BMH.

30. James Cullen Witness Statement, BMH.

31. Fearghal McGarry, *The Rising, Ireland Easter 1916*, p. 243.

32. John O'Reilly Witness Statement, BMH.

33. RIC Yearly Report, 1916, pp. 10-11.

34. Galligan Witness Statement, BMH.

35. John O'Reilly Witness Statement, BMH.

36. Charles Townsend, *Easter 1916 – The Irish Rebellion*, p. 274.

37. RIC Report on the Sinn Féin or Irish Volunteer Rebellion.

38. John O'Reilly Witness Statement, BMH.

39. Galligan Witness Statement BMH.

40. Paul Galligan to Eugene Galligan, 29 November 1917.

41. Galligan Witness Statement, BMH.

42. Dáil Debates, Dáil Éireann, Volume 87, 2 July 1942, Committee on Finance. Adjournment – Enniscorthy Military Service Pensions.

43. Paul Galligan to Monsignor Eugene Galligan, 29 November 1917.

44. RIC Yearly report, 1916.

Chapter 4

'Hell with the Lid Off' – Imprisonment, 1916-1917

Paul Galligan and another 64 Irishmen were imprisoned in Dartmoor Prison and afterwards in Lewes and Parkhurst Prisons from May 1916 until June of the following year. For them the experience was a severe trial, but also in a sense, a continuation of the fight they had begun during Easter week. During the Rising, they had shown the willingness of the Volunteers to fight and to die for Irish independence. In the prisons, they would struggle to resist British attempts to treat them as criminals and to vindicate their vision of themselves as Irish soldiers.

Paul Galligan's last residence in Ireland, before being sent to England to serve his five -year sentence of hard labour, was Mountjoy Prison in Dublin. Before he left he had an emotional encounter. His fiancé Peg Hyland, had heard he was imprisoned in the city, and 'hunted for me for two days, at the risk of losing her post'. Finding him in Mountjoy must not have been much of a consolation. She was not in the Movement and had done 'all in her power to prevent me [from taking part in the Rising] and was always at me to give up what she knew would lead to trouble and her last words to me was imploring me to follow her advice, which I did not do'.

'When she found the word "convict" stamped on me for five years, she took it bravely and said she would wait for me.' Peg's loyalty led Paul Galligan to reveal the couple's engagement to his father. 'I am sure we will be very happy, for a girl who makes such a sacrifice for a boy must be truly sincere.' However, their relationship did not survive after his spell in prison.[1]

Most of the 1,400 people interned after the Easter Rising were sent to a prisoner of war camp at Frongoch in Wales, previously occupied by captured Germans. It says something about Galligan's prominence among the leaders of the rebellion that he, along with 64 others, was instead selected for detention in a maximum security prison at Dartmoor.

Galligan was taken under guard by a detachment of Dublin Fusiliers, 'good fellows, who treated us well', on a ferry from the North Wall to Liverpool. He remembered that 'the escort were very decent and treated us well and bought refreshments for us'. Some of the Irish soldiers even sang rebel songs on the crossing.

Others' experience of British troops had not been so benign however. Eoin MacNeill told Galligan on the journey about how, in Arbour Hill Prison, guarded by soldiers with fixed bayonets, he was paraded in front of the men who were digging the graves of the executed leaders. 'This, he said, was an attempt to frighten him into writing a confession.' They left writing material in his cell and shortly afterwards, MacNeill began writing. The guards thought that they had won the battle but on entering the cell to read MacNeill's confession, they were angered to read that MacNeill, the University professor of history, had merely jotted down some notes on Irish history.[2]

Most of those who had been sent to Dartmoor would have been shot as leaders of the Rising had the British Prime Minister, Asquith, not cut short General Maxwell's executions. The most senior prisoners were Éamon de Valera, the only Volunteer commandant in Dublin who had not been executed, Eoin MacNeill, the head of the Volunteers and William Partridge, the most senior surviving officer of the Citizen Army. Alongside Galligan were the other Wexford leaders, Seamus Doyle, Seamus Rafter, Robert Brennan and Seán Etchingham. The other prisoners included the leaders of the Rising outside Dublin; Thomas Ashe, who had led the Rising in county Meath and Seán MacEntee whose Louth Volunteers had seized the village of Ardee.

It is something of an irony then, that the leaders of both the IRB and the IRA in the coming guerrilla struggle of 1919-1921, Michael Collins and Richard Mulcahy, rose to prominence among the prisoners at Frongoch – testimony to the dangers for the British of bringing together so many activists in what they later called 'a university of revolution'. But it was the 120 prisoners condemned to penal servitude – half in Dartmoor Prison, half in Portland – who did the hardest time.

Dartmoor

Dartmoor prison is a hulking, grey mass of brick, surrounded by low green hills and beyond that, mile after mile of Devon moorland. The prison complex is a perfect circle, with an assembly square at the centre and both administrative buildings and six-storey prison blocks radiating outwards, like spokes in a wheel. Around it is a high stone wall, topped with barbed wire.

The prison was a maximum security facility, where the criminals considered most dangerous served sentences of penal servitude. It had been built in 1809 to house French and American prisoners of war. In an incident known as the 'Dartmoor massacre' in 1815, the Royal Navy Captain in charge of the prison had opened fire on the inmates, killing seven and wounding 31. Some 1,500 French and American soldiers died there from 1809-1816, as a result of the cramped conditions, harsh treatment, malnutrition, and disease. Legacies of those days were still visible in 1916. Wexford Volunteer officer Seamus Doyle found etched in his cell the name of French soldier, 'Henri Journee, 1803'.[3]

Dartmoor became a criminal prison from 1850 and while the mortality rate was not what it was in its days as a prisoner of war camp, the conditions there were still brutal. Prisoners were not allowed to speak or interact with other inmates and were allowed to write and receive only one letter every four months.

Inmates could be flogged with a cat o'nine tails or birched for breaking these rules. They would also be confined to what was then known as the 'cachot', or punishment block, for up to 10 days and be fed only two-thirds of their normal Daily ration. Flogging of prisoners with the birch was still practised at Dartmoor until the 1950s. More common by 1916 though, was to punish rule-breaking by three days in solitary confinement on nothing but bread and water. The psychological pressure that this regime exerted on the prisoners – particularly the isolation and inadequate food – was enormous.[4]

The conditions at Dartmoor almost inevitably provoked either despair or violent rebellion among the prisoners – and not only among Irish nationalists. In 1932 there was a mutiny among the inmates, sparked off by protests about the poor food, and many parts of the buildings were destroyed by fire.

Paul Galligan later wrote to his brother of his time in the prison: 'Yes, we got hell in Dartmoor, their very means as well as the influence and power of a full Masonry Prison Board was used to break us up. I have often heard this war [the First World War] spoken as "hell with the lid off", but the originator of this expression never put a week in with us in Dartmoor jail or he would have added "and all the past and present generations of English men trying to devour 65 Irish convicts and could not".'[5]

'The Drudgery and Humiliation of Prison Life'

Everything about penal servitude was designed to reduce the prisoner to a state of powerless obedience. On arrival at Dartmoor Prison the Irish prisoners were stripped naked, lined up for inspection and searched. Éamon de Valera later told a friend that 'the shyness of the Irish lads gave the impression of their being cowed'.[6]

The next step in subsuming the convict's individuality into their role as a prisoner was the prison uniform. Each convict was issued with convict clothes which included a jacket, underpants, long stockings, leggings, nailed boots, shoes, cap and a smock for wet days. All of the clothing was stamped with the broad arrow – the British Government's brand for prison material. The Volunteers were housed in the West Wing of the prison and kept in single cells. Their cells were spread over the four floors. Galligan was on the top or third floor, next to those of MacNeill, Seán MacEntee and Kerry Volunteer leader Ted Brosnan. They were not allowed to communicate with each other but they were at least, Galligan recalled, 'kept separate from the ordinary criminals'.[7]

Conditions in the cells were spartan. There was no heating in the cells and bedding consisted of a thin mattress placed on the cell's floorboards, only three inches from the concrete floors. They were issued with two blankets (three in the winter) and a bedspread. The cold was so severe that many of the prisoners developed acute lumbago or back pain. The food was 'an ordinary prison diet and most days very poor' and prisoners were not allowed to receive food from outside.

They exercised every morning before work, but again no communication was allowed with any of the other incarcerated Volunteers. Their work, making mail bags, also had to be done in silence. They were permitted one bath and haircut per week.[8]

The silence and solitude of Dartmoor was what affected the prisoners most. Paul Galligan wrote to his brother in September 1916: 'I feel quite lonely at times for no matter how strong a willpower you may possess, you will find your thoughts drifting back to times that are past . . . but this is only what you might expect when you consider the long and dreary hours we have to ourselves.'[9]

There was strict censorship of Galligan's few letters from Dartmoor and as a result, they contain little or no political content. He told his father, perhaps so as not to worry him. 'I have never felt in better spirits nor do I remember enjoying better health.' But after his transfer to Lewes, where conditions were less strict, his real feelings came out: 'Yes we have seen the drudgery and humiliation of prison life and not only have we tasted the gall of the convict but were made to drain the cup to the dregs. Often as I paced my cell at night I asked myself, is there a just God in heaven?'[10]

After the Easter Rising, Galligan had written that he felt indifferent to whether he was executed or not. And there are signs that during his imprisonment, these darkest of thoughts returned to haunt him: 'I always read with horror the sad incidents of suicide but I will never read of suicide in future without pity and compassion for I know the battles those souls had to fight and it is only our Irish Catholic faith that brought us unsullied through it all.'[11]

The winter was especially difficult: 'Light came in through a muffed pane of glass and from a small gas lamp, lit from the outside of the cell. It was almost impossible to read with this light and during the winter months the cold was so severe that if you wanted to read you had to wrap the blankets around your feet and legs.'[12] Seamus Doyle remembered of Dartmoor, 'Prison life with its rule of perpetual silence was drab and dreary . . . memories of home often brought loneliness and longing.'

Paul Galligan sent letters to his father, mostly on personal matters, above all trying to settle up his debts in Dublin and Wexford. Galligan it seems clear, was a diligent saver in his years in Dublin (it may have helped that he neither drank nor smoked) and he had lent substantial sums that he now asked his father to collect. One of his most pressing concerns was a loan of £55 at 6 per cent interest he had given to one Mrs. Fagan of Henry Street, after her son emigrated to Australia, 'when she was sorely in need of it'.

It seems Mrs. Fagan did not pay him back however. In March 1917, Galligan reflected ruefully: 'As regards Miss Fagan, I know from my own experience that writing would do no good. . . . Yes Dad, I answer with you, God save me from my friends. I have learned many things during the last twelve months. Experience sometimes bought dear but now the brass is separated from the gold.'[13]

In September 1916, Peter Galligan made the journey to Dartmoor to see his son in person. Apart from occasional letters and visits from family, one of the only consolations for the Volunteer prisoners, overwhelmingly Catholic, was religious services. Paul Galligan wrote to his brother: 'I go to communion every Sunday and assist at Benediction every Sunday evening . . . we raise our hearts to Mary and thank her for that priceless gift she gave our forefathers and which now brings such sweet sympathy and compassion for our souls.'[14]

Another diversion was reading. Seamus Doyle remembered that there was a good library in the prison and that prisoners could request books by writing their titles on a slate in their cells. Paul Galligan 'read and re-read' two volumes of Thomas Carlyle's *The French Revolution, A History* – a vivid, stylised, nineteenth century portrayal of the revolution of 1789. Galligan may have seen a parallel with the Easter Rising in Carlyle's description of the storming of Bastille: 'On then Frenchmen, all that have hearts in your bodies! Roar with all your throats, of cartilage and metal, ye sons of Liberty!'

He might also have agreed with Carlyle that revolt was sometimes better than living in degradation. Carlyle wrote in the 1830s that whereas the French san cullotte (working class revolutionary) had died for a promise of 'Hope and Faith of Deliverance' that turned out to be in vain, it was worse to have been starving Irish 'sans potato' [without potato] who died without protest; 'it was bitter for him to die famishing, bitter to see his children famish'.

People were no longer starving to death in Ireland in 1916, but what may have impressed the Irish revolutionary most was Carlyle's idea that a determined minority, what he called, 'heroes', could push events in their direction – moulding the hopes and aspirations of people into ideologies or 'formulas'. The Easter Rising had, of course, been just such an attempt.[15]

The treatment of the Irish prisoners, according to Seamus Doyle, was not unusually harsh by the standards of the draconian regime at Dartmoor. He recalled: 'As the warders came to know us, they seemed to realise that we were not of the type to which they had been accustomed and, with a few exceptions, they did not seem to persecute us.'[16]

The Irish were, in many ways, different from the other inmates at Dartmoor. They did not see themselves as criminals who had done something wrong and were receiving punishment. Rather, they were patriots, temporarily imprisoned by 'the enemy'. So rather than a mass of individuals, they were, even in the highly isolating conditions of Dartmoor, a collective, with their own identity and leadership. This made resistance to the prison system possible, even if only in occasional displays of defiance. 'Although there was no overt act of revolt on our part in Dartmoor,' Seamus Doyle recalled, 'the situation was always tense.'[17]

At the head of the prisoners was Éamon de Valera, whom the prison governor referred to as 'a real firebrand and fanatic . . . he is decidedly a "personality" and the others seem to look up to him as their leader'.[18] De Valera's military leadership of the Volunteers at Boland's Mill during the Rising had been open to criticism. He had refused to sleep for six nights in the Mill, which he spent pacing furiously up and down. Some of his orders had been contradictory, for instance ordering his men to burn Westland Row train station and then changing his mind and getting them to put out the blaze under fire from British snipers. He had also failed to reinforce a small outpost just streets away at Mount Street bridge that was faced with a frontal assault for two days, resulting not only in the loss of those men but in British troops crossing the canal into the city centre.[19]

But in prison, there was no doubting either de Valera's charisma or his stature among the prisoners. Paul Galligan recalled later: 'His fight for his fellow prisoners, to my mind, marked him out as our future leader.'[20] From the very start, according to what de Valera told Frank Gallagher in 1928, 'after the indignity of the first personal search when convicts are publicly stripped naked, he decided that a fight was necessary'.[21]

When Eoin MacNeill arrived in the prison – in the same batch of prisoners as Paul Galligan – de Valera had his first opportunity for a confrontation. The prisoners were lined up in two rows for the morning inspection when MacNeill came down the stairs. Seamus Doyle remembered: 'Commandant de Valera, who was standing at the end of one of the lines, stepped out on our front and gave the order: "Irish Volunteers, eyes left". We gave the salute. There was commotion among the warders and Commandant de Valera was taken away.'[22]

De Valera's own recollection was that 'they were not expecting it and did not answer smartly but at least the gauntlet had been thrown down'. He was hauled before the Governor. 'Why did you do that?' he was asked. 'To salute my commander in chief in the proper manner,' de Valera replied. 'Do you not know that any such action is mutiny, the most serious crime a prisoner can commit and that flogging is the punishment?' De Valera's reply summed up the stand he was taking: 'I know nothing about that, I only know we are soldiers and owe respect to our commanders.'[23]

What really stuck in Paul Galligan's memory however, was another occasion when de Valera sacrificed himself for another prisoner. 'In the opposite cell to de Valera there was a huge big man called Phil McMahon . . . he was always hungry as the prison food was insufficient for him.'[24] Other accounts state that the prisoner was Jack McArdle and that he had been put on three days ration of bread and water for some minor infraction.[25] Either way, 'de Valera somehow discovered that McMahon had insufficient food and . . . threw a small loaf of bread across to McMahon'.

His action was spotted by the warders and de Valera was again taken to see the Governor where he argued that 'the bread was his and he did not require it and he had the right to give it to any man who required more food'. De Valera was put in the punishment block or 'cachot' on bread and water for three days. Shortly afterwards, he and Desmond Fitzgerald were transferred to Parkhurst Prison on the Isle of Wight.[26]

Lewes

In 1916 right through until the Treaty of 1921, British coercion was enough to embitter and anger Irish nationalists but not consistent enough to terrify them into submission. So it was in December 1916, when David Lloyd George replaced Asquith as British Prime Minister. Lloyd George released all of the internees at Frongoch and transferred those at Dartmoor and Portland and other high security prisons to the lower security facility at Lewes Prison in Sussex. Lloyd George was anxious to assuage Irish-American as well as Irish opinion in an effort to get the United States into the First World War.

For Paul Galligan, this meant a transfer to Lewes, hand-cuffed on 20 December. 'I arrived here last night after a long train journey. I think about 250 miles and was not sorry when we reached the end.'[27] Galligan later recalled: 'Here [in Lewes] conditions were the same except that we were allowed to talk and associate during exercises.' The word 'except' betrays the fact that this made a world of difference to the Irish prisoners. Now free to associate, they could organise collective resistance to the prison system. Significantly, also, 'de Valera returned to us and we were all glad to see him'.[28]

For the first time since their arrest, the prisoners could exchange experiences of the Easter Rising. 'I met all my Dublin comrades which were in Portland and as it was the first day we were allowed to talk. I need hardly say we had a lot to say to each other and on the whole there was a great comparing of notes.'[29]

On St. Patrick's Day the prisoners had a 'general communion', where the 120 Irish prisoners marched in military formation to mass. 'It was glorious to see one hundred and twenty all garbed in [prison uniform], and on which was stamped the arrow, the official colour and mark of the convict. On both breasts was sprig of shamrock. Some wore a Patrick's harp worked in green white and orange . . . as they filed past with military step and manly bearing which twelve months of prison life has not affected.'[30]

On 29 April, the first anniversary of the Rising, they held a memorial service for the Volunteers who had died in Easter week, 'those noble souls, the purest and best of Irish manhood and although we feel lonely and sad for such comrades yet we cannot regret them, they have led a noble life and died a glorious death'.[31] The prisoners also organised Irish language and Irish history classes.

Galligan, in a letter to his brother,[32] expressed his contempt for British popular culture, an attitude as much formed by Irish Catholic social morality as republican separatism.

Two factors helped to lift Paul Galligan's mood in early 1917. One was the spring weather. 'Thank God the cold and misery of winter is passing and we are glad to see a little sunshine again.'[33] The other was the resurgence of radical nationalism in Ireland.

In early 1917, Sinn Féin, a party previously associated with radical nationalism but not with the Rising, was taken over by republicans and veterans of the Rising and won two by-elections, in North Roscommon and South Longford. Referring to the election of George Plunkett (father of one of the executed leaders of the Rising) in Roscommon, Galligan wrote to his father: 'Yes it was a magnificent victory for Plunkett, 3,200, it is significant.'

Public opinion, prodded by the repression of the Rising but also discontent at the failure to implement Home Rule and the threat of conscription into the British Army for the World War, was shifting in the separatists' favour. Paul Galligan wrote mockingly of 'our friend from Swinford [Irish Parliamentary Party figure John Dillon] . . . seems to be getting hard knocks these days'.[34]

Also in February 1917, Paul received his first letter from his brother, Monsignor Eugene, who pledged his support to Paul and the Rising of 1916. This was a major relief to Paul as he had been uncertain of his brother's position on the insurrection. The blessing from a priest of their actions was always welcomed and this particular letter was passed from Volunteer to Volunteer, 'you could see the eye brighten and the head rising, for each of them knew that Ireland had a good and true friend in Australia'.

In Lewes prison, de Valera upped the stakes in the stand-off with the prison authorities, demanding either political status for the prisoners or their release. When this was refused, on 28 May 1917, he issued orders to the prisoners to refuse to do prison work. According to Seamus Doyle, before the strike could go ahead, permission first had to be got from the Volunteer leadership in Dublin. Their assent was conveyed to the prisoners in a telegram via the prison chaplain, Dr McLoughlin. De Valera, Doyle recalled, told them, 'we would no longer consent to being treated as criminals and we took orders from him, instead of the warder-in-charge'.[35] 'To fail,' he told the prisoners, 'would be dishonour to the dead – to Ireland. Friends and Foes are watching you. It must be death rather than surrender.'[36]

The protest soon turned violent. The men were locked in their cells and smashed the glass and furniture, 'everything breakable' recalls Seamus Doyle. After ten days of protest, the British Home Office decided once again to break up the prisoners and they were dispersed to different prisons around Britain. Galligan remembered that before leaving Lewes, each man promised he would not work and this was strictly observed in all prisons. They were refused exercise and many of them placed their mattress on the corridor outside their cell and spent their day reading books.

Paul Galligan, by this time suffering from ill-health and in the prison hospital, was sent to Parkhurst on the Isle of Wight.[37] During transfer, the prisoners were handcuffed to each other in parties of six or eight. He was not the only prisoner to fall sick during the prison experience. William Partridge, the Citizen Army officer, died shortly after his release in 1917.

Release

At Parkhurst, Galligan was, for the first time, mixed with ordinary English criminals. In his memories of the time, taken down thirty years later by the Bureau of Military History, Galligan talked fondly of 'the occupant of the next cell to mine . . . a man named McMahon who had been sentenced to be hung for the "tunnel murder" in England. I found McMahon to be a charming fellow, very courteous and cheerful and in great sympathy with us Irish.'[38]

In his letters at the time, though, Galligan referred with disgust to the 'British imbecile convicts', 'diseased convicts' and 'the lowest of criminals, thieves and pickpockets'. 'So bad was this prison,' he reported, 'that we refused to use the lavatories so prevalent was venereal disease.'[39] McMahon had, however, spent ten years in prison and was a good source of news and of writing materials ('impossible to get in a penal prison').

Paul Galligan's stay in Parkhurt was relatively short – no more than a month. In late June 1917, Lloyd George announced an amnesty for the remaining Irish Volunteer prisoners. It was a goodwill gesture ahead of an all-party 'Irish Convention' he planned for that summer to try to negotiate a way out of the deadlock over Home Rule. Galligan, originally sentenced to die, had served a year and two months of his five-year sentence.

In Parkhurst, Galligan was slipped a note by his neighbour McMahon telling him the Irish were about to be released. 'McMahon asked me would we kick up a row when leaving and I said, "No we will leave singing 'God Save Ireland'." He said, "Wherever I am I will sing it with you".' The following morning the eight Irish prisoners marched out of the prison gates singing the Fenian anthem dating from the 1867 rebellion:

> God save Ireland, said the heroes
> God save Ireland, said they all
> Whether on the scaffold high
> Or the battlefield we die
> Oh, what matter when for Erin dear we fall

'The last sight I saw,' Galligan remembered, 'was McMahon at the cell window, also singing, true to his word.'[40]

Homecoming

After a brief stop in Pentonville Prison, where the Volunteers prayed at the grave of Roger Casement, executed there the previous August, they were sent by train to the port at Holyhead and on by ship to Dublin. Their mood was ebullient, singing the rebel songs, 'Kelly the boy from Killane', 'Steady Boys, Step Together', and 'The Soldier's Song' – which nearly provoked a brawl with British soldiers who were also on board.

Paul Galligan had been spared the experience of many rebels of being abused and jeered at by hostile Irish crowds at the end of the rebellion. His memory was, 'when we had left Dublin for Dartmoor, the people seemed to be getting sympathetic towards us; now they seemed to be with us wholeheartedly'. At Westland Row train station there was 'a tumultuous reception from the people for the returning prisoners', who were then taken to a breakfast and reception in Maloney's Hotel in Gardiner Street.

Paul Galligan's time in prison had been very hard for him in many ways but it had not at all dimmed his enthusiasm for the separatist cause – indeed the acute sense of oppression in prison and the solidarity of the prisoners' experience probably strengthened it. On the same day he arrived back in Dublin, 'An Official appeal for the Republic was prepared'.

The Easter Rising itself was conceived of as something of a last throw by the separatists, a desperate attempt to resurrect the idea that Ireland might demand independence rather than ask for Home Rule. Now for the first time, partly as a result of the Rising but also because of the breakdown of Home Rule and the demands of the War, there was a prospect of swinging the majority of the Irish people behind the idea of an independent Republic.

Endnotes

1. Paul Galligan to Peter Galligan, 1 June 1916.

2. Galligan Witness Statement, BMH

3. Seamus Doyle Witness Statement, BMH. Note: Doyle gave two statements, on the Rising and one on prison. His imprisonment at Dartmoor is WS 1,342.

4. Robert Walsh, 'Dartmoor: The Prison That Broke the Body and then the Soul', *Crime Magazine*, 16 May 2010.

5. Paul Galligan to Monsignor Eugene Galligan, October 1917.

6. Coogan, Tim Pat, *De Valera, Long Fellow, Long Shadow* (1993), p. 80.

7. Galligan Witness Statement, BMH.

8. Galligan Witness Statement, BMH.

9. Paul Galligan to Monsignor Eugene Galligan, 26 September 1916.

10. Paul Galligan to Monsignor Eugene Galligan, 6 April 1917.

11. Paul Galligan to Monsignor Eugene Galligan, 4 May 1917

12. Galligan Witness Statement, BMH.

13. Paul to Peter Galligan, 16 June 1916 and 6 March 1917.

14. Paul Galligan to Monsignor Eugene Galligan, 26 September 1916.

15. Carlyle, Thomas, *The French Revolution*, Abridged and Edited, by A.H.R. Ball, Cambridge 1930.

16. Seamus Doyle Witness Statement, BMH.

17. Seamus Doyle Witness Statement, BMH.

18. Diarmuid Ferriter, *Judging Dev* (2007), p. 30.

19. Tim Pat Coogan, 1916, *The Easter Rising*, Phoenix, London 2005, pp. 124-125, Paul O'Brien, *Blood on the Streets: The Battle for Mount Street*, p. 86.

20. Galligan Witness Statement, BMH

21. Tim Pat Coogan, *De Valera*, p. 80.

22. Seamus Doyle Witness Statement, BMH.

23. Tim Pat Coogan, *De Valera*, p. 80.

24. Galligan Witness Statement, BMH.

25. Tim Pat Coogan, *De Valera*, p. 81.

26. Galligan Witness Statement, BMH.

27. Paul Galligan to Peter Galligan, 20 December 1916.

28. Galligan Witness Statement, BMH.

29. Paul Galligan to Peter Galligan, 20 December 1916.

30. Paul Galligan to Monsignor Eugene Galligan, 16 April 1917.

31. Paul Galligan to Monsignor Eugene Galligan, 4 May 1917.

32. Ibid.

33. Paul Galligan to Peter Galligan, 6 March 1917.

34. Paul Galligan to Peter Galligan, 6 March 1917.

35. Seamus Doyle Witness Statement, BMH.

36. Tim Pat Coogan, *De Valera,* p. 84.

37. Galligan Witness Statement, BMH.

38. Ibid.

39. Paul Galligan to Monsignor Eugene Galligan, 14 October 1917.

40. Galligan Witness Statement, BMH.

Chapter 5

The Birth of a Republic, 1917–1919

'Ireland has gone Sinn Féin mad'

While Paul Galligan was in prison, the political climate in Ireland had changed dramatically. From majority support for Home Rule and the Irish Parliamentary Party, the public's support had swung to the separatists in Sinn Féin. This was partly down to the power of the Easter Rising itself, the powerful example of which had inspired a new generation of young militant nationalist activists. Paul Galligan, back in his native Cavan in October 1917, wrote to his brother Eugene, 'God bless the men who died in Easter week, our casualties, was [sic] only 60 plus 16 executed, a total of 76, but if you saw Ireland today you would say it was worth it all for it has gone Sinn Féin mad.'[1]

On 20 August 1917, at Clones, County Monaghan, Paul Galligan along with Sinn Féin leader Arthur Griffith addressed what the local newspaper the *Anglo-Celt* described as a 'Monster Meeting'. Galligan was introduced to the enthusiastic crowd as a veteran of the Rising. The watching RIC recorded that he told his listeners: 'Fellow Gael, I accept your cheers not for myself but for the men who fell in Easter week and who lie in Glasnevin, but also for my comrades who were executed in Kilmainham Gaol and who lie in the Barrack Yard at Arbour

Hill and the only prayers that reach their sacred bones are the blasphemous oaths of the British soldiery. . . . I say to you men with all sincerity, if you wish to remain Volunteers, there is a warm reception for you in the ranks of the Volunteers and with that reception you will receive a rifle and 100 rounds of ammunition.'[2]

Galligan's reception in Monaghan is a very clear indication of the rapid change in public opinion after the Rising. Just after the rebellion itself, the RIC County Inspector in Monaghan reported that, 'The feeling of the people generally towards the rebels at the time was that they were guilty of a mad act as the rebellion was causing great loss of life and destruction of property and had no chance of success.'[3]

At the rally in August 1917, a local priest, Fr. Daly, called Galligan 'a splendid young man that was not afraid to look into English guns on Easter Week'.[4] Arthur Griffith took the opportunity of the meeting at Clones to outline his strategy of Irish MPs withdrawing from Westminster and unilaterally declaring Irish independence: 'The sending of representatives to the British Parliament, which was a recognition of England's right to rule Ireland, had been the basic error of Irish politics for the last hundred years, because it turned the thoughts and the minds of the people from their own strength in their own country, and taught them to put their trust in a foreign legislature, where the Irish members were outnumbered six to one.'

Griffith told the crowd, that by contrast, 'The Sinn Féin policy was clear and distinct: That the Irish people were by national right and international right, a free people, that anything that obstructed that freedom was tyranny, and must be removed, and the way Sinn Féin proposed to remove the tyranny was by non-recognition of English authority in Ireland.'[5]

Some of the new post-Rising generation of republican activists, such as future IRA leaders Ernie O'Malley, Liam Lynch and Eoin O'Duffy, had no previous involvement in separatist politics, but were radicalised by the rebellion itself and its aftermath. O'Malley, for instance, a medical student in Dublin, joined the Volunteers shortly after the Rebellion.[6]

Liam Lynch, a former Hibernian, joined the Volunteers in Middleton when he saw local republicans being dragged away by the RIC in the wake of the rebellion.[7] O'Duffy, previously secretary of the Gaelic Athletic Association and Gaelic League in Monaghan, made the short jump from cultural to armed nationalism after the Rising.[8]

This new generation would supplement the older activists like Michael Collins, Richard Mulcahy and Paul Galligan, who had served their 'apprenticeship' in the IRB, the Volunteers, the Rising and in British prisons.

For Galligan, the prison experience, though it had 'left a stamp on me that time will never efface',[9] had only hardened his commitment. In Dartmoor, he told his brother, he used to dream of 'the figure of Eireann . . . her face marked with sorrow on which was still the trace of recent tears. But in her eyes with that new look of hope which you only see on a face of one, who battling for life see hope after hope fade away and who at the eleventh hour see in the distant horizon aid and succour. On her lips was a smile that brought a thrill to my heart for it was the smile of victory. As she passed I seemed to hear her say, "after prison, freedom". Such is a dreamer's dream.'[10]

The representation of Ireland as suffering woman, dreaming of delivery from oppression, was very old, dating back to, at least, the Irish language poetry of the seventeenth century and common in the literature of the Gaelic revival of the early twentieth century. But it shows how powerful the prison experience was for Galligan. It had crystallised his understanding of 'freedom' into something very concrete. Freedom now meant personal freedom from prison and police raids, as well as simply Irish independence.

Given his total immersion in the cause of Irish independence, it is perhaps not surprising that Paul Galligan's relationship with Peg Hyland, who he had decided to marry in late 1915, came apart. Hyland had never been in the separatist movement and, despite promising to stand by Galligan while he was in prison, did not share his commitment to the cause.

At some time, either while Galligan was still in prison or shortly after his release, the couple broke up.

While on the run in 1918, Galligan would often be welcomed at the safe house of Liam Coyle. Paul became increasingly interested in Liam's eldest daughter, Mollie who he
would eventually marry in 1922. Tellingly, unlike Peg Hyland,
she was also a republican activist and a member of the Cumann na mBan.

'Redmond is a Man of the Past'

For the population at large, the Easter Rising and its suppression was not the only catalyst for the swing away from the Parliamentary Party and towards Sinn Féin. Equally, if not more
important was failure to implement Home Rule and the threat
of Britain imposing conscription on Ireland for the Great War.

Home Rule had, in theory been passed through the British
parliament back in 1914, but, in the face of armed unionist opposition, postponed for the duration of the war. In the immediate aftermath of the Easter Rising, Asquith sent David Lloyd
George to Ireland to try to negotiate an agreed Home Rule deal
with the Irish Party and the Unionists. In July 1917, not long
after Paul Galligan returned to Ireland, the new government
led by Lloyd George himself tried again, with an 'Irish Convention' involving the Irish party and the Ulster Unionists.

Not only were these attempts at solving the 'Irish Question' unsuccessful, but the prospect of the partition of Ireland,
which was brought up at the talks and agreed to by John
Redmond as the price for Home Rule, outraged nationalists
all over Ireland. In County Wexford, for example, the police
reported: 'The feeling of the people was strongly against the
proposed Home Rule Settlement by way of partition.'[11]

The other great boost for the separatists was the threat of
conscription. Back in 1914, Irish nationalists, encouraged by
Redmond, had enthusiastically joined the British Army for the
Great War. By 1917, this enthusiasm had all but vanished. The
Irish units had suffered heavy casualties at the fronts and the
war had also meant rising prices and taxes. Recruitment in Ire-

land had slowed dramatically. A total of 44,000 Irishmen had enlisted in 1914, 45,000 followed in 1915, but this dropped to 19,000 in 1916, 14,000 in 1917 and 11,000 in 1918.[12] The British government had imposed conscription in Britain itself in 1916 to fill the quotas of troops desperately needed for the western front and pressure was mounting on it to extend this to Ireland.

But in Ireland, aggrieved at the failure to implement Home Rule and angered by the repression of the Rising, there was no longer a widespread sense of patriotic duty to Britain. Rather, all nationalists, from the ITGWU trade union, to Sinn Féin, to the Irish Party and the Catholic Church pledged to resist conscription. New Sinn Féin clubs and Volunteer companies sprang up around the country. The Irish Volunteers saw their numbers swell from less than 10,000 to over 100,000 by 1918, while the Redmondite National Volunteer organisation faded away.[13]

By late 1917, Paul Galligan reported to his brother: 'Nothing but the full independence of Ireland will satisfy the Irish people. Redmond is a man of the past and his policy is only supported by a dwindling minority. . . . Sinn Féin clubs, at least two and in some cases three, are already established in every parish, this in itself will give you an idea of what Sinn Féin has accomplished.'[14] Sinn Féin won by-elections in Longford, Roscommon and Clare in 1917. Two of the new MPs, Joe McGuinness and Éamon de Valera, had been in Lewes prison with Paul Galligan.[15]

There was, as yet, no sign that the separatists planned another bout of armed resistance, but renewed confrontation was already in the air. At the homecoming of Paul Galligan and the other post-Rising prisoners, they were cheered through the streets of Dublin and spoke at a mass rally along the Quay side. Cathal Brugha, who had been badly wounded in the Rising, gave an inflammatory speech, for which he was placed under arrest by a watching RIC inspector. A vicious riot ensued, in which the arresting policeman was felled, mortally wounded, with a blow from a hurley stick.[16]

The republicans also had new martyrs. In August 1917, Thomas Ashe, a leader in 1916, and President of the IRB Supreme Council, was arrested for a 'seditious' speech and died on hunger strike in September after forced feeding. Ashe had occupied the cell next to Paul Galligan in Dartmoor and Galligan wrote after his death: 'The poor fellow, I knew him well. We were in Dartmoor and Lewes together and he was a fine type of man in every sense of the word, but his death was a second, "Easter Week 2 in terms of the change of public opinion.'[17]

There is no mistaking the air of determination in Galligan's correspondence: 'We are at last marching to freedom, glorious freedom, this time the might of England cannot stop our march for neither money nor jobs can buy us. All we want is Ireland free to act and work out her own salvation, in other words an Irish Republic and for that we are willing to die, if again necessary.'[18]

Forging a New Movement

The years 1917–1918 saw a coming together and re-forging of a new republican movement. Sinn Féin, which had been founded in 1905 had never before been a republican party – Arthur Griffith's original idea had been for an independent Irish parliament and was prepared to accept British-Irish 'dual monarchy'.[19] In 1917, though, Sinn Féin was taken over by the republicans and committed itself to the withdrawal of Irish MPs from Westminster and the foundation of an Irish Republic. Its new President was the man Galligan had identified in Dartmoor Prison as a natural leader, Éamon de Valera. Its strategy in the short term was to seek international recognition of the Irish case from America and, when the Great War ended, from the post-war peace conference. Representations were also sent to revolutionary Russia, since overthrowing the Tsar in February 1917 itself under republican government.[20]

Galligan, along with other released prisoners such as Éamon de Valera and his Wexford comrades, Seamus Doyle and Seán Etchingham, put his name to an open letter to the

American President and Congress in July 1917. It began, 'We, the undersigned, who have been held in English prisons, and have been dragged from dungeon to dungeon, in heavy chains, cut off since Easter Week, 1916', and appealed to 'the Government of the United States of America, and the Governments of the free peoples of the world, to take immediate measures to inform themselves accurately and on the spot about the extent of liberty or attempted repression which we may encounter. . . . We, the undersigned, are officers (just released from English prisons) of forces formed independently in Ireland to secure the complete liberation of the Irish Nation.'[21]

All separatists were colloquially known as 'Sinn Féiners' but Paul Galligan had never previously been a member of the actual Sinn Féin party. After his release from prison, though, he campaigned actively for the party as well as the Volunteers in his native Cavan.

In October 1917, Galligan attended the first Convention of the new Sinn Féin in Dublin as delegate for South Leitrim. Over 1,700 delegates from 1,000 clubs, representing 250,000 members took a unanimous decision to demand an Irish Republic at the peace conferences and to 'demand nothing less as we want now to completely sever our connection with England'. Galligan wrote to his brother, 'it made you feel proud to be a Sinn Féiner to see all the fine young fellows that were there and it would give you food for thought if you stood in the balcony and looked down on the noble, intellectual faces that were below . . . one thought that struck me most was, "if the governing of this country was in those men's hands what would we be in five years".'[22]

The Volunteers in Cavan

Parallel to the political movement was the revival of the Volunteers as a paramilitary force. As before the Rising, this was closely directed, behind the scenes, by the IRB. The previous leadership of the Volunteers and IRB were either dead, or in the case of Eoin MacNeill and Bulmer Hobson, discredited in the eyes of veterans of the Rising. Hobson was frozen out completely from the separatist movement and Michael Collins had to persuade some of the more vengeful IRB men from court-martialing and shooting him for his part in trying to stop the Rising. MacNeill was left in place, in theory, head of the Volunteers, but in fact was by-passed by IRB men such as Richard Mulcahy – who assumed the job of Chief of Staff – and Collins as Director.[23]

The post-1917 Volunteers was also a much larger organisation than before and Mulcahy and Collins tried to either swear prominent local Volunteers into the IRB or place members of the Brotherhood at the head of Volunteer units. At the Volunteer Convention of October 1917 (just after the Sinn Féin Convention), Paul Galligan was appointed northern volunteer representative and was instructed to organise the Irish Volunteers in Counties Cavan and Leitrim. In one way, Galligan was a strange choice, as he had not lived in Cavan for over ten years. However there was a lack of experienced activists in Cavan and no doubt Galligan's IRB connections and his reputation as a veteran of the Rising also counted in his favour.

Cavan had been, up to 1917, a county dominated by the Irish Party and its auxiliary, the Ancient Order of Hibernians. When the Volunteers split in 1914 over Redmond's pledge to support the British war effort, almost all the local Volunteers joined Redmond's 'National Volunteers'. A handful of IRB circles did exist. Francis Connell, a local activist, was a member of one in Bailieboro, while James Cahill recalled another in Cavan town. The only active Irish Volunteer company, however, was in Ballinagh (the area coincidentally, around the Galligan homestead) and that had less than 100 men. It had been set up by a man named Archie Heron in 1915.[24]

Such a small group could probably have done little in the Rising but in any case, due to Eoin MacNeill's countermanding order, the Bailieboro men stayed at home.[25] Apart from Paul Galligan, only one Cavan man actually fought in the Rising, one N.T. Caldwell, who was taken prisoner at the GPO in Dublin. A Cumman na mBan activist, Una O'Higgins, was also arrested in possession of dispatches from Cavan addressed to the Rising's leaders and sentenced to three months in Armagh Gaol.[26]

As elsewhere, it was the post-Rising repression that gal-vanised the growth of the republican movement in the county. In May, June and July 1916, Cavan was scoured by patrols of the Iniskilling Fusiliers and the 36th Ulster Division, who carried out arrests all over the county.[27] If the authorities had set out to antagonise nationalists in Cavan, they could hardly have devised a better plan than this – to employ predominant-ly Protestant, Unionist units (the 36th was recruited directly from the Ulster Volunteers) to carry out wholesale arrests in an area where no Rising had occurred.

When the last prisoners were released in June 1917, the RIC noted that Sinn Féin took off in the county, growing from four clubs with a mere 108 members to 53 clubs and 2,623 members by December of that year.[28] By the end of 1918, with the impact of the anti-conscription campaign, the police reported of Sinn Féin that 'its strength in comparison with the adherents of the Irish Parliamentary Party would be about 3-1'.[29]

Sinn Féin and the Volunteers were movements of young and less wealthy people previously excluded by the Irish Party establishment. The RIC reported that in Cavan they were 'chiefly supported by the young men and voters who got the franchise under the recent act'.[30] Paul Galligan both acknowledged and mocked this depiction in an ironic aside to his brother, 'we are only poor uneducated and ill-advanced young men'.[31]

In July 1918, Arthur Griffith was elected for East Cavan in a by-election after the death of Sam Young, the IPP incumbent. The by-election saw the first physical confrontations for the Cavan Volunteers with the police and rival political parties. Under Galligan, they paraded in defiance of the post-Rising ban on drilling. More importantly, they also provided security for Sinn Féin canvassers from the police and from the hostile local members of the Ancient Order of Hibernians and the Orange Order. Francis Connell, a Volunteer in the Bailieboro company recalled guarding Sinn Féin speakers with concealed revolvers and shotguns, carried openly.

Volunteer James Cahill remembered that 'we were constantly on protective duty during the by-election. The Ancient Order of Hibernians was ferocious in their attacks on members of the Sinn Féin organisation. Occasionally they were assisted by the Orangemen. . . . Frequently Hibernians or Orangemen would conceal themselves behind walls or hedges and attack us with stones as we cycled past.' The RIC, according to Cahill, did not intervene in such affrays unless it looked like the Volunteers were winning. 'We were very fortunate that none of our members got seriously hurt.'[32]

In practice, though, the Volunteers tended to win such confrontations with rival nationalists and hostile unionists, if only because they carried firearms and were prepared to use them. Francis Connell, for instance, recalled one occasion in which his Volunteer company, doing election work over the county border in Monaghan, were attacked by 'Hibernians, Orangemen and Ulster Volunteers, armed with stones, bottles, scythes and pitchforks', near Carrickmacross. Things were looking bad for the republicans until they produced their revolvers and fired over the heads of their attackers, who rapidly dispersed.[33]

In the celebrations after the by-election victory, Volunteer James Cahill became involved in a brawl with the police, head butting one as he tried to arrest a fellow Volunteer. Cahill was charged with assault and the young republican firebrand was all for refusing to recognise the court. He was dissuaded by his commander, Paul Galligan. No doubt, in his years of activism, Galligan had learned a thing or two about how to avoid prison terms. He ordered Cahill to recognise the court and to plead guilty to common assault. 'Paul's orders saved me from six months imprisonment and I was let off with a fine of 10 shillings, which I never paid.'[34]

The RIC, unhappy with the lenient verdict, pressured Cahill's employers in Cavan town to let him go. They did at first, although a visit from the local Volunteers made them reconsider. Afterwards, Cahill moved to Dublin, where from 1920, he became a fearsome guerrilla operator in the IRA Active Service Unit.

'Let the Military Do Their Own Dirty Work'

Paul Galligan, shortly after his release from prison, wrote to his brother that he would rather die than go back. 'There will be no prison, no jail, "Freedom or Death!".'[35] But due to his work with Sinn Féin and the Volunteers in Cavan, he soon found himself again on the wrong side of British law.

This was becoming increasingly arbitrary as the strength of the separatist movement grew and the stand-off over conscription went on. In neighbouring Monaghan, Eoin O'Duffy was arrested for organising a GAA match, which had been proclaimed as an 'illegal assembly'. At the same time the Orange Order's annual parades were allowed to go ahead. The Redmondite press raged at the 'imbecility' of Dublin Castle's policy.[36] In May 1918, alleging a 'German plot' between the 'Sinn Féiners' and their enemies in Europe, the British issued arrest warrants for hundreds of leading separatists, among them Paul Galligan.

While there had been contacts between the Germans and Irish republicans since Easter 1916, the charge was essentially an excuse to round up militant leaders after mass protests against conscription in April 1918. Edward Shortt, the new Chief Secretary, all but admitted as much: 'We do not pretend that each individual has been in personal active communication with German agents, but we know that someone has.' Some 70 suspects were arrested, but many more, including Michael Collins, evaded capture.[37]

Galligan went on the run in Cavan to avoid arrest but just prior to the July by-election, he broke cover to go to Mass at the village of Crosserlough with another Volunteer named Hugh Maguire. On their way to the church, the two noticed a constable Kelly watching them. All three knew each other and exchanged glances but Kelly made no move to arrest them. When Galligan and Maguire emerged from Mass, however, Kelly and another constable, Mulligan, were waiting for them.

Maguire recalled: 'Galligan asked them to produce their warrant for his arrest, the police said they had not got a warrant but the military had, to which Galligan replied, "let the military do their own dirty work". And we got on our bicycles and cycled off to Ballyjamesduff.'[38]

The scene can be imagined. Two locals, one a hero of the Easter Rising, campaigning for a successful candidate in an election, facing off against the forces of a state (albeit Irishmen themselves) that was increasingly discredited by its arbitrary arrests of nationalist activists. And all of this occurred in the one place where everyone in a small rural community was bound to see it; in the church yard after Mass. Unsurprisingly, 'a nice hostile crowd gathered around us [Maguire and Galligan] and the two constables, I suppose, thinking discretion the better part of valour, did not interfere with us'.[39] The British Army surrounded Maguire's home that afternoon, but he had the good fortune not be there.

The 'forces of order', however, caught up with Paul Galligan shortly afterwards and arrested him at his home, not long after Griffith's victory in the by-election. Peter Galligan wrote that his son was arrested at 3.30 in the morning, 'by 8 police and 12 soldiers'. All the signs are that the repression of the separatist movement compromised the legitimacy of the British administration more than it harmed the republicans. Peter Galligan told his son Eugene: 'Paul committed no crime beyond being an ardent worker for the Sinn Féin cause. Indignation is running very high here at present owing to the high-handed action of the Irish government.'[40]

The 1918 Elections

In November 1917 Paul Galligan was already writing to his brother that 'with the exception of about two seats, we will win all the parliamentary seats at the next election and we are preparing hard and fast for it for I am of the opinion that peace is near at hand and with peace of course comes a general election.'[41]

He was a little premature in his prediction of the war's end, but in December 1918, only a month after the end of the Great War on 11 November, the United Kingdom held its first ever general election with universal suffrage. Every man over 21 and every woman over 30 was entitled to vote, regardless of property. In this election, Sinn Féin buried the Irish Parliamentary Party. It won 73 seats out of 105 and just under 50 per cent of the vote.[42] Sinn Féin's percentage of vote would have been considerably higher except that in many constituencies the IPP did not even field candidates. Redmond's party retained only six of their 84 seats.

In West Cavan Paul Galligan, although interned in Reading Jail, was elected unopposed, as was Arthur Griffith in East Cavan. Elsewhere in the country, the election saw considerable violence, mostly between the nationalist rivals, the republicans and Hibernians, but as there was no contest in Cavan, the county remained quiet. Perhaps the Sinn Féin victory in the July by-election had already knocked the heart out of the local Redmondites.

The fact that so many Sinn Féin candidates were unopposed seems to modern eyes to partially discredit their victory in 1918, but in fact it had been the most democratic election in Irish history up to that point. In 1910, 64 out of 103 constituencies were uncontested, compared to 27 out of 105 in 1918.[43] Under the new franchise the electorate was almost tripled, from 700,000 to over two million, and in contested constituencies there was a turnout of around 68 per cent.[44] Sinn Féin had received a resounding endorsement of their policy of abstentionism and independence.

Galligan wrote to his girlfriend Mollie Coyle from Reading jail: 'Cavan has been a surprise to us all and as Napoleon would say, "it has covered itself in glory", and in future we can hold our heads high. Cavan is the "Gap of the North" and the lead that Cavan has given will be nobly followed by Ulster and some of the Ulster results will surprise even you Mollie.'[45]

Despite Galligan's optimistic predictions, though, the rest of Ulster was the one black spot for Sinn Féin in the country. The unionists in the nine northern counties won more than twice as many votes as Sinn Féin (234,376 to 110,032), and in the six counties that would later make up Northern Ireland, the unionist majority was still larger. Within two years, these six north eastern counties would have their own secession – but from the rest of Ireland rather than from Britain.

Sinn Féin, true to their election manifesto, refused to take their seats in Westminster and instead declared their own Irish parliament, the Dáil. The first meeting of Dáil Éireann occurred on 21 January 1919 in the Round Room of the Mansion House (the residence of the Lord Mayor in Dublin). The Declaration of Independence asserted that the Dáil was the parliament of a sovereign state called the 'Irish Republic', and so the Dáil established a cabinet and elected the 'President of Dáil Éireann'. The first temporary president was Cathal Brugha. He was succeeded, in April, by Éamon de Valera.

Paul Galligan was not there, however. He was one of the 35 deputies who were described as being 'imprisoned by the foreigners' (*fé ghlas ag Gallaibh*). Another four were listed as being 'deported by the foreigners' (*ar díbirt ag Gallaibh*) in the records of the new parliament. In fact, only 27 of the 105 elected deputies were present (two were absent for undisclosed reasons and another 37 were unionists or IPP members).

On the same day, two RIC policemen were escorting a consignment of gelignite explosives at Soloheadbeg in County Tipperary when they were ambushed by a party of Volunteers led by Dan Breen, Seán Treacy and Seamus Robinson. The two policemen were shot dead, their weapons and explosives seized. No one in the Dáil – or even in the Volunteer leadership - had ordered the attack, and many were uncomfortable with its ruthlessness. Richard Mulcahy, the Volunteer Chief of Staff, said it was 'tantamount to murder', but in hindsight the ambush was later recognised as the opening shots of the Irish War of Independence.[46]

In 1916, the rebels had, effectively, represented no one but themselves. In 1919, Paul Galligan and his comrades were in a very different position – that of an elected Irish government trying to defend itself from obliteration by the anti-democratic forces of the British Empire. This clash would lead to three years of guerrilla warfare, a conflict quite different from the 'stand-up fight' of 1916.

'This Awful Pestilence'

Before leaving 1918 it is worth also mentioning an event that is prominent in virtually all the contemporary accounts: the epidemic that hit Ireland in the winter of 1918. The year is justly remembered in Ireland for the election that led to the formation of the Dáil, but for people at the time, an equally pressing concern was the outbreak of the 'Spanish flu'. The epidemic is estimated to have killed 40 million people worldwide and in six months infected some 800,000 people in Ireland and killed about 23,000.[47]

The flu hit both the Galligan home and that of his girlfriend Mollie Coyle. He wrote to her: 'I was very very sorry to hear that this awful pestilence which the English language calls "flu" visited your home and it was sad to see all except my Bridie laid up and I am delighted to hear that it has passed over and that all are on their feet once more, but I expect a little weak still, but everyone should be most careful for a time yet, as it is in a relapse all the danger is.'[48] Bernard Brady, a Cavan Volunteer, caught the flu while attending the Sinn Féin Convention in October 1918 and was hospitalised for three months.[49]

In their annual report, the RIC noted the impact of the epidemic in virtually every county. In Cavan they reported that 'the disease carried off a great many and affected nearly every household'.[50]

Endnotes

1. Paul Galligan to Monsignor Eugene Galligan, 14 October 1917.

2. Speech Notes Recorded by the Police, CO 904/23/3, The National Archives, Kew, Richmond, Surrey, TW9 4DU, England.

3. Fearghal McGarry, *Eoin O'Duffy: A Self-Made Hero*, p. 23.

4. Speech Notes Recorded by the Police, CO 904/23/3, The National

Archives, Kew, Richmond, Surrey, TW9 4DU, England.

5. 'A Monster Demonstration', *Anglo Celt* 13/10/17.

6. Ernie O'Malley, *On Another Man's Wound*, pp. 48-50.

7. Peter Hart, *IRA and its Enemies*, p. 205.

8. Fearghal McGarry, *Eoin O'Duffy: A Self-Made Hero*, p. 26.

9. Paul Galligan to Monsignor Eugene Galligan, November 1917.

10. Paul Galligan to Monsignor Eugene Galligan, 4 May 1917.

11. RIC Yearly Report 1916.

12. David Fitzpatrick 'Militarism in Ireland', in Thomas Bartlett and Keith Jeffery, eds., *A Military History of Ireland,* p. 388.

13. ME Collins, *Ireland, 1868-1968*, pp. 241-242.

14. Paul Galligan to Monsignor Eugene Galligan, 17 October 1917.

15. Fergus Campbell, *Land and Revolution, Nationalist Politics and Land in the west of Ireland, 1891-1921,* p. 197.

16. T. Ryle Dwyer, *Tans, Terror and Troubles: Kerry's Real Fighting Story,* p. 116.

17. Paul Galligan to Monsignor Eugene Galligan, 15 November 1917.

18. Paul Galligan to Monsignor Eugene Galligan 14 October 1917.

19. Marie Coleman, *County Longford and the Irish Revolution,* p. 3.

20. Galligan Witness Statement, BMH.

21. Intrigues Between Sinn Féin Leaders and the German Government, CAB/24/117, The National Archives, Kew, Richmond, Surrey, TW9 4DU, England. See Appendix I.

22. Paul Galligan to Monsignor Eugene Galligan, 15 November 1917.

23. Peter Hart, *Mick, The Real Michael Collins*, p. 143.

24. Witness Statements, Francis Connell, James Cahill and Seamus MacDiarmada, BMH.

25. James Cahill Witness Statement BMH.

26. Seamus MacDiarmada, Witness Statement BMH.

27. Seamus MacDiarmada, Witness Statement BMH.

28. RIC Yearly report, 1917.

29. RIC Yearly Report 1918.

30. Ibid.

31. Paul Galligan to Monsignor Eugene Galligan, 29 March 1918.

32. James Cahill, Witness Statement BMH.

33. Francis Connell Witness Statement BMH.

34. Ibid.

35. Paul Galligan to Monsignor Eugene Galligan, 15 November 1917.

36. Fearghal McGarry, *Eoin O'Duffy: A Self-Made Hero*, pp. 35-36.

37. Charles Townsend, *Easter 1916 – The Irish Rebellion*, p. 340.

38. Hugh Maguire Witness Statement 1,387, BMH.

39. Ibid.

40. Peter Galligan to Monsignor Eugene Galligan, 7 July 1918.

41. Paul Galligan to Monsignor Eugene Galligan, 15 November 1917.

42. Michael Laffan, *The Resurrection of Ireland: The Sinn Féin Party, 1916-1923*, p. 164.

43. Charles H. E. Philpin, *Nationalism and Popular Protest in Ireland*, p. 415.

44. http://www.ark.ac.uk/elections/h1918.htm

45. Paul Galligan to Mollie Coyle, 19 December 1918. The 'Gap of the North' refers to battles fought by the Irish chieftain Hugh O'Neill against the English along the Ulster border in the sixteenth century.

46. Michael Hopkinson, *The Irish War of Independence*, p. 115.

47. Ida Milne, Is History Repeating? The Spanish flu of 1918 http://puesoccurrences.com/2009/06/02/history-repeating-the-spanish-flu-of-1918/

48. Paul Galligan to Mollie Coyle, 19 December 1918.

49. Bernard Brady Witness Statement, BMH.

50. RIC Yearly Report, 1918.

Chapter 6

Paul Galligan's War of Independence, 1919–1921

'A Declaration of War'

For Paul Galligan, the War of Independence was a clash between the democratically created Irish Republic and the despotic, illegitimate British regime. In October 1919, he was taken before what he called 'a trumped up court marshal in which every iota of evidence was forgery'.[1] Asked if he had anything to say, he told the court: 'At the commencement of this court-martial I asked you had you any moral right to try me. You took me here by force, you try me surrounded by rifles and bayonets and therefore your only authority is force.'[2]

When subsequently brought to Belfast Jail and told he would not be afforded the status of a political prisoner, he told the Governor: 'This is a declaration of war and it is now a fight between you, representing the British Government and I representing the Irish Government and the Irish will win. . . . I refuse to do anything, work or otherwise which would make me a criminal.'[3]

Galligan spent most of the conflict (January 1919 to July 1921) in prison. He was released from internment for the so-called 'German plot' in March 1919, but arrested again for illegal drilling in August of that year. Temporarily released for ill health in September, he refused to report back to prison and went on the run until he was arrested again, and in the process shot and wounded, in September 1920. He spent the rest of the conflict imprisoned in the maximum security prison at Lincoln in England.

In between his stints in prison, Galligan worked to organise both Sinn Féin and the Volunteers in western Cavan – a combination of electoral canvassing, operating an alternative system of government and guerrilla warfare.

The War in Cavan

If one were to look at the events of the period in County Cavan as a period of conventional 'war', one might conclude that not much happened in the area. In total, the local Volunteers (from 1919 known as the Irish Republican Army or IRA) killed three RIC officers and wounded several more. Several police barracks were attacked but none taken. Two civilians were shot dead by the IRA, one as an alleged informer the other in a house raid. Three IRA Volunteers were killed in the County and another Cavan IRA man was killed just over the county border in Leitrim.[4] A total of nine deaths. This was a low casualty rate, not only by the standards of, for instance, County Cork, where 523 lost their lives, but also judged against the neighbouring counties of Longford and Monaghan, in both of which about 30 were killed, or Leitrim, where 17 died.[5]

But looking only at the low body count is to misunderstand profoundly the nature of the conflict and its impact both on participants and on the wider society. The Sinn Féin movement in Cavan, largely under Galligan, worked first to win political support, winning the 1918 election and then the County Council elections in the summer of 1920. Parallel to this, it set up an alternative system of government. The existing court system was replaced, in Cavan as early as 1917, by Sinn Féin or Dáil courts. The function of the Volunteers was largely to enforce the rulings of these courts and to ensure, by intimidation or otherwise, the public ostracism of the British institutions.

By and large, they achieved this. The RIC in Cavan reported by October 1920 that 'Sinn Féin . . . dominated the life of the county'.[6] While Cavan Volunteer Seán Sheridan recalled: 'The Volunteers had the co-operation of the majority of the general public. The remainder, perhaps through fear, were not openly antagonistic.'[7]

The response of the state forces was draconian but usually less than lethal. Hundreds of Volunteers were arrested and had their homes raided. Sinn Féin courts were broken up, their activists harassed and their houses sometimes burned. For the republicans, as Galligan wrote to his brother in December 1919, 'we are living under a reign of terror'.[8]

The IRA in Cavan, whether due to a lack of arms, or disorganisation with so many of their leaders being arrested, or perhaps, as some complained, a lack of ruthlessness, made only halting steps to redress the physical domination by Crown forces of the county. There was a great deal of blocking of roads and cutting of communications but only sporadic attacks on Crown forces in the County – some of them mounted by units from outside Cavan.

At a personal level, the struggle had great personal costs for Paul Galligan. Not only did he suffer physically – shot in the arm and suffered from ill health in prison – he was also forced to re-live the 'hell' of maximum security prison that he had first experienced at Dartmoor, with its enforced isolation, silence and crushing discipline.

1919 Arrest and Hunger Strike

As early as November 1917, the Sinn Féin 'state within a state' was beginning to make its presence felt in County Cavan. Paul Galligan reported to his brother that a 'Sinn Féin Post Office' had been set up, to get around the British censorship and seizing of mail.[9] In and around the same time, the Sinn Féin Clubs in Cavan passed a motion to set up courts 'to whom all disputes shall be referred . . . to whom any aggrieved party may appeal and that . . . shall have the entire force of the Sinn Féin movement, financially or otherwise, to reinforce the awards;

. . . and thereby deny law costs to the Crown or any traffic at all avoidable in English courts.'[10] By October 1917 these were operating in Ballyconnell, Kingscourt and Swanlibar. The Dáil courts were formally instituted in early 1920, but in Cavan they effectively regularised what was happening already.

Much of the work of the Volunteers in Cavan was enforcing the rulings of these assemblies – effectively replacing the RIC as police. Seán Sheridan remembered: 'The Volunteers had the co-operation of the vast majority of the people, something the RIC could never get. There had always been a void between the people and the RIC, and since the rise of Sinn Féin this had become accentuated.' Petty criminals were arrested and made to work for farmers in another battalion area, others were made to pay compensation to their victims.[11]

At the same time, the Volunteers enforced a boycott of the RIC. Some locals who took Sinn Féin to the British courts over their occupation of a hall, got a visit from members of the Bailieboro Volunteers which 'compelled them to withdraw proceedings'.[12] Later, as of September 1920, IRA members also enforced a boycott of Belfast goods in retaliation for the loyalist attacks on Catholics in that city.

The Volunteers in January 1919 administered an oath to their members, in which they swore to be loyal to the Irish Republic and the Dáil.[13] From this point onwards, they considered themselves the soldiers of the Irish Republic and began to refer to themselves as the IRA. They also began collecting the 'Republican loan' to subsidise the revolutionary regime. Paul's brother in Australia, Monsignor Eugene Galligan, was an advocate of the Irish Cause and in April 1920 he sent Paul £100 to support the Republican struggle.[14]

They had, however, very few weapons. For this reason, another common Volunteer activity throughout 1919 was raiding houses for arms. Perhaps naturally the first to be raided were those that were hostile to Sinn Féin. Volunteer Bernard Brady recalled, 'we had to raid the houses of all those opposed to us and Sinn Féin generally, and seize their guns'.[15]

According to Francis Connell, 'we raided all the houses in the area for arms, including those of the Ulster Volunteers'.[16] Such raids generally yielded only shotguns however.

On 15 June, 1919, when three RIC officers came upon Paul Galligan drilling some 80 Volunteers in a field at Gortaree, none of them were armed with anything more lethal than a hurling stick. Performing military drills had been made illegal in Ireland after the Easter Rising for anyone other than those enlisted in the British military.

Galligan was commanding his men when one of them called his attention to the three watching policemen. RIC Sergeant John Flanagan later testified, 'I heard the instructor [Galligan] remark they would soon put us out of that'. Galligan formed up his men and gave the commands: 'About turn,' 'charge', and when they approached the road, 'at the road, fire!' Since the Volunteers did not have any guns as yet (or at any rate were not carrying any), a volley of stones looped through the air at the policemen.

The RIC, by contrast, routinely carried carbines and revolvers and Sergeant Flanagan told the stone throwers to 'desist or be prepared for the consequences'. As Galligan formed up his men to march them away, Sergeant Flanagan demanded his name. Galligan mockingly asked the policeman, 'was he not in receipt of a good salary?' ('Fairly good,' Flanagan replied). Shortly afterwards, at the Feis at the Cavan County fair, Flanagan had 'the Instructor' identified for him as Peter Paul Galligan by another RIC sergeant, John Kerr.[17]

On 27 June 1919, the County Inspector of County Fermanagh sought an order from General Headquarters in Parkgate, Dublin to arrest Peter Paul Galligan, a 'well known local extremist'. A directive to arrest Peter Paul Galligan was issued by the General Officer Commanding-in-Chief, Ireland and to detain him in Belfast for court-martial.[18] Galligan was arrested at his home by armed police and troops on 14 July, and was convicted at court-martial of illegal drilling and incitement to attack the RIC. He was sentenced to 12 months hard labour at Belfast Gaol.

Included in 'Secret' and 'Confidential' documents issued by GHQ in Parkgate was clear instruction to Headquarters in the Northern District about what evidence should be included and omitted. In particular, direction was given as to which witness statements should be included and the presentation of the evidence. Witness statements sent to GHQ for review were amended. The letters were signed by Lieutenant-Colonel H. Toppin on behalf of the Major-General in charge of Administration. In one of his letters he states: 'The passages marked in blue pencil in the summary should be omitted at the trial and the evidence of Sgt. Kerr and Constable Somersett should be given at the trial in the following form – that Sgt. Flanagan made a certain statement to them regarding one of the persons present at the Feis at Cavan, whom they recognised as Peter Paul Galligan, and identify as the accused now present. Anything in the nature of hearsay must be carefully avoided.'

Each of the four witness statements of Sergeant John Flanagan, Constable Patrick McMackin, Sergeant John Kerr and Constable Christopher James Somersett were amended. Any reference to hearsay was removed. While it was quite normal for GHQ to review evidence and witness statements before a court-martial, it's very evident that the British Authorities were determined to secure a successful conviction against Paul Galligan. After the court-martial, GHQ advised the Speaker of the House of Commons of the arrest and outcome of the court-martial of elected member, Peter Paul Galligan.

Testifying against a Volunteer leader was becoming a risky business, however. Galligan remarked somewhat coyly to his brother, 'the police who swore against me in my court martial never returned to their barracks nor have they been seen since'.[19]

He did not spend long in jail on this occasion however. In Belfast, on being told that he was to be treated as a common criminal, he refused to work or exercise with the other prisoners. The Governor charged him with insubordination and put him in solitary confinement for three days on bread and water.

Galligan responded by refusing all food and going on hunger strike for ten days, 'refusing to take criminal food'.[20]

Perhaps mindful of the recent death of Thomas Ashe on hunger strike, the British, having 'tried everything' to break Galligan off his strike, released him for a month on 27 August on the grounds of ill health. It may also have been significant that the Dáil had passed a resolution of protest at his detention, and on 26 August Michael Collins wrote to Galligan providing him with a copy of the resolution passed by the Dáil earlier that week.

His release was reported in *The Irish Times*:

> '*HUNGER STRIKERS RELEASED. – Messrs. P.J. Berrills, P. Galligan, M.P.; and Samuel Herron, who have been on hunger strike in Belfast Jail have been released.*'[21]

Galligan was supposed to report back to Belfast after a month, but had no intention of doing so. After he arrived back from a conference of Sinn Féin Ulster representatives in Omagh, 20 police raided his home. Fortunately for him, 'some important business called me away' and he was not in. From then on, though, he had to lead a clandestine existence – 'circumstances will not allow me to stay at home for long'.

Galligan's attitude was still bullish though. It seemed clear to him that the republicans were winning the moral confrontation. He wrote to his brother: 'Day by day the Irish case is getting stronger. Day after day we are beating England into a corner from which there is no escape and by the time this reaches you, England will have made an offer of a settlement to us but she will find different staff to deal with than the Imperial putty [the IPP] which Ireland had been sending to England for some time.'[22]

'The Biggest Fight of All'

Being on the run meant that the Galligan home was raided no less than seven times by the police in the coming months. Paul Galligan wrote that 'we are living under a regime of terror, worse than even the Russians or the Poles passed through when the despotism of the Czar was at its worst'.[23] British repression was hurting the wider movement also. Galligan reported: 'Dáil Éireann is suppressed and so is all our papers for publishing prospectus of the Republican Loan.'[24]

In November 1919, the British banned the Dáil, Sinn Féin and a host of other nationalist organisations. Most of the republicans' political leadership was now in prison. Éamon de Valera, the President of the Republic, was in America. Peaceful means appeared to have run into a wall of repression. This left the way open for Michael Collins and Richard Mulcahy to launch a guerrilla war.

Collins had always been convinced that such an eventuality would be necessary. In late 1919 he argued, 'All ordinary peaceful methods are ended and we shall be taking the only alternative actions in a short while now.'[25] In early 1920, on the orders of Collins and Mulcahy, there was a wave of attacks on RIC barracks around the country. In this new phase, unarmed confrontation with the RIC, like Galligan's at Gortaree, would give way to much deadlier encounters.

In Cavan, though, Paul Galligan was still preoccupied with political matters. He wrote to his brother: 'We are now preparing for the biggest fight of all – the County Council [elections]. . . . It will be a wonderful test of our strength and by the time you get this letter, Ireland will have won the greatest victory. She will have chased out the old gang of selfish imperial crawlers and have replaced them by a body whose ambition is the prosperity of the country and who will not be afraid to do the right thing at the right time.'[26] Galligan's optimism was not misplaced: between Sinn Féin and Labour (at this stage close allies of the republicans), the separatists captured all the urban and County Council seats in Cavan.[27]

The IRA guerrilla campaign however was slow to take off. In March 1920, local IRA men, apparently on Galligan's orders, held up the mail van with the old age pension money which amounted to £75. Galligan dispatched a subordinate named Hugh Maguire to Dublin to buy weapons from where he returned with seven rifles and several automatic pistols –

still not enough for large scale attacks but a big improvement on the shotguns and revolvers they had had up to then.[28]

IRA GHQ was suspicious of the robbery, however, presumably considering that it was bad publicity for the movement. Hugh Maguire thought it was for this reason that they were cautious about sending any more arms to Cavan for the rest of the war.[29] At Easter 1920, the Cavan Volunteers joined in a nationwide operation in burning abandoned RIC barracks – the police having a month earlier evacuated them in favour of larger, more defensible buildings.

In the summer of 1920, the IRA in Cavan suffered a number of setbacks. Firstly, several prominent activists, like Paul Galligan from the Ballinagh area, were arrested, including Thomas Fitzpatrick and Peadar Cowen. Worse was to come. In May, an IRA party from Galligan's West Cavan unit tried to ambush two RIC men at a fair in Crossdowney to take their weapons, though 'strict orders were given by the battalion OC [Galligan] that no lives were to be taken in the attempt'.

This was probably unrealistic. In fact, when the police were challenged, they opened fire with their pistols. In a shootout, one of the Volunteers, Thomas Sheridan, was shot and mortally wounded; his brother Paul and one of the policemen were also injured. The police, who swore they would kill the other Sheridan brothers if the wounded sergeant died, set fire to the thatched roof of the Sheridan house that night. The roof fell in but the house itself was saved by the efforts of the neighbours.[30] Sheridan was buried at Ballinagh, 'with full military honours'. Seán Sheridan, his brother, recalled: 'A firing party of Volunteers armed with revolvers fired three volleys over his grave. The RIC did not interfere with the funeral and kept indoors while it was taking place.'[31]

In August, another Volunteer, Joe McMahon (originally of Clare) was killed in an explosion in Cavan town while testing homemade grenades. Another, Pat Roche, was badly injured.[32] But most damaging for the local IRA were the constant raids and arrests. The local RIC were by now backed up by an infantry detachment of the British Army, the Norfolk Regiment, as well as the often brutal new paramilitary police recruits known as the 'Black and Tans', recruited from British ex-servicemen.

The IRA intelligence officer Seamus MacDiarmada recorded that his company 'lost 11 men in one sweep alone'. Where there was evidence to convict them, men were given sentences of up to ten years. Many others were interned in camp opened at Ballykinlar, County Down. MacDiarmada recalled that the arrests meant that the Sinn Féin courts either 'ceased' or went underground.[33]

'Such Savagery I Never Witnessed'

In early September 1920, the British forces finally captured Paul Galligan. His father Peter had been unwell and Paul, compassionately but perhaps unwisely, stayed in the family home for two weeks to nurse him back to health.

Someone alerted the RIC and Army, who descended on the house to arrest Galligan. Galligan always knew that returning to the homestead was a risk, but his father was suffering from a severe sick stomach and he felt compelled to return home. Paul's desire to look after his father was further heightened by the departure of his brother Jimmy for the USA, after a bitter row with his father, leaving no other family members at home.

On 7 September 1920, ten armed Black and Tans raided neighbour Bernie Brady's house in Corlislea in search of Paul Galligan. After the British party left the house, Brady's youngest daughter Nellie went to Drumnalaragh to warn Galligan. The child was going up Mattie Conlon's Hill, quite close to Galligan's house, when the British lorries passed her by.

The armed police and troops burst into the house. Peter Galligan wrote: 'Paul was in the kitchen just after our tea. Paul rushed out the back door pursued by four armed soldiers who fired several shots at him at short range. He got as far as Mc-Cann's garden gate and while in the act of opening the gate a rifle bullet went right through his arm. So he was easy prey for the bloodhounds. The bullet went right through the fleshy part of the arm between the elbow and wrist. Such savagery I never witnessed. They wouldn't give me time to have his wound dressed or allow him into the house but dragged him into the motor and drove to Cavan.'[34]

Peter Galligan was clearly shaken by the incident. 'I am not very strong myself for some time and poor Paul, my sole consolation being now snatched from me is a cruel blow. But God in his mercy will sustain us all. I would give all I possess in this world or every hope to have in it, to be a young man again (God's will be done).'[35]

The front page of the *Anglo Celt* reported:

WEST CAVAN M.P. SHOT

ARREST OF MR. PAUL GALLIGAN

*On Tuesday evening at 6 pm police from Cavan and Bal-
linagh went to the residence at Drumnalaragh, Ballinagh,
of Mr. Paul Galligan, T.D. for West Cavan, who has been
on the run since his release after hunger-strike twelve
months ago, and as he was hurriedly leaving the house, a
shot was fired which took effect in his left arm. Mr. Galligan was then taken into custody and brought to Cavan
police barracks. The same night he was conveyed by military lorry to Belfast.*[36]

For Paul Galligan it was the start of yet another bout of imprisonment – his fourth. He was taken into custody and brought to Cavan police barracks. The same night he was conveyed by military lorry to Belfast. Galligan was transferred to Liverpool prison and afterwards to Lincoln prison.

Cavan, 1920-1921

The arrests of senior figures like Galligan hurt the Cavan IRA and their Intelligence officer Seamus MacDiarmada recalled that by late 1920 it was 'very unorganised'. After Galligan's arrest, Charles Fitzpatrick replaced him as Battalion Comman-dant.

IRA GHQ in Dublin tried to re-organise the Cavan Brigade by splitting it between three newly-created commands – the Cavan-Cootehill area was put in the 5th Northern Division under Monaghan IRA leader Eoin O'Duffy, Galligan's Ballinagh-Arvagh area was put under the command of Longford leader Seán MacEoin in the 1st Midland Division and the Bailieboro-Virginia companies were allocated to the 1st Eastern Division.[37]

In September 1920, the North Longford flying column killed two Black and Tans and attacked a police barracks at Arvagh, with the co-operation of the local Cavan units. In December, another policeman was shot dead in an ambush at Swanlibar and an attack was planned on Ballyjamesduff barracks, but called off at the last minute. Mollie Coyle of Latnadrona cycled to Belturbet to collect mines and explosives for the attack. Mollie Coyle was later to marry Paul Galligan in 1922.

By and large, the Cavan units confined themselves to cutting communication and blocking roads. For instance, the RIC reported in October 1920: 'On the night of 8-9-20 the telephone wires connecting Ballinagh RIC with the Post Office were maliciously cut. The motive is resentment at the re-arrest of Paul Galligan, M.P. who has been evading arrest for the past 12 months.'[38]

The Volunteers also clandestinely enforced Sinn Féin's political hegemony. Hugh Maguire remembered raiding the houses of men who were about to join the RIC to warn them off. In raiding the house of one aspirant RIC member, the man, Rooney, a Protestant, was shot in the leg, with a shotgun. The leg later had to be amputated.[39]

When the Ulster Special Constabulary (effectively a unionist militia) was formed in late 1920, Francis Connell recalled raiding the homes of both Protestants and Catholics who joined, sometimes prompting exchanges of gunfire.[40]

In May 1921 IRA GHQ tried to draft in a flying column from outside Cavan – a scheme which ultimately ended in disaster. Seamus McGoran, an IRA organiser from Belfast, was sent to Cavan and arranged to import one of the Belfast IRA's two Active Service Units, of 13 men, who were joined by about ten locals.

Their camp at Lapinduff mountain, however was discovered within three days by Crown forces – apparently after some loose talk in a local pub by some of the Belfast men. In local Volunteer Seán Sheridan's opinion, 'the position was to my mind, a very bad one. It was on top of a hill which stood up like a pimple in the surrounding countryside'. The column was surrounded by a British military and RIC party of 70-80 men and after a three-hour fire fight in which one IRA man was killed and another wounded, all were captured. At least one British soldier was also injured. The IRA men (who included Patrick Smith, a future Sinn Féin and Fianna Fáil TD for Cavan) were sentenced to death but reprieved by the 11 July truce.[41]

The Lapinduff affair was a severe setback for the IRA in West Cavan. Aside from its effect on morale, most of the Brigade's weapons were lost in the fiasco and the flying column was never re-organised. One more IRA Volunteer, Stan McEntyre, was 'killed on military manoeuvres', according to the IRA memorial in Cavan, in June 1921. Another, Michael Baxter, died at Selton Hill in Leitrim, in an incident reminiscent of the Lappinduff fight, along with six other Volunteers, in March of that year.[42]

The IRA in Cavan was not very ruthless about hunting down and shooting spies and informers. Seamus McKenna, one of the Belfast men captured at Lapinduff, thought that 'our presence was undoubtedly betrayed to the enemy', and he complained that 'no effort was made to locate and dispose of the informer'.[43] Many of the Cavan men maintained that there were no spies in their County, Hugh Maguire, for instance, said that 'no spies were shot in the area and I doubt if such existed'.

One Volunteer claimed that the RIC in Cavan did not need informers such was their local knowledge. Indeed, an RIC constable told the Belfast IRA men, 'we know every inch of ground and I was born and reared not far from here'.[44] But the RIC's information was too accurate for there not to have been some level of informing. James Cahill, for instance, the Dublin IRA fighter from Cavan, returned to his parents' home near Cavan town for only a few hours in May 1921 before it was raided by troops and Black and Tans.[45] It seems more likely that, rather than Cavan being informer-free, the Cavan Volunteers did not have the heart to kill local civilians who talked to the police.

There was one rather tragic exception to this however. The body of a shoemaker from the Mallaghoran area named Patrick Briody was found by the RIC on 25 May 1921, about three weeks after the fight at Lapinduff. The RIC had often visited his shop and the IRA suspected him of passing them information.

One Volunteer, Seán Sheridan, said that he was, 'arrested, tried by court-martial and shot as a spy'. But another, Hugh Maguire thought that he was raided for serving the RIC in defiance of the boycott of the police. He refused to join the boycott and, 'in the attempt to persuade him forcibly he, unfortunately was killed'.[46]

A similar and equally ugly incident took place on 12 June, when a 78 year old Protestant clergyman, John Finlay, was shot dead in an IRA raid on his home at Brackley, near Bawnboy. The killing was mentioned in the British House of Commons, where Hamar Greenwood, the Chief Secretary for Ireland, called it 'a diabolical outrage'.[47] However, according to a local historian: 'One member of the Volunteer party which raided Brackley House told me that Dean Finlay's death was an accident and not murder. He himself was present when the shot that killed the Dean was accidently discharged from a gun.'[48]

On the 10 July, just a day before the truce which ended the war, the Bailieboro Volunteers attacked the RIC barracks in that town – 30 strong, armed only with shotguns. The attack was beaten off with two IRA wounded and two more captured.[49]

The War of Independence in Cavan was of a low intensity. Arrests and intimidation by both sides were more common than killings. By a purely military standard, the Crown forces were in the ascendancy, but in a political conflict of this type, such measures are largely irrelevant. The Volunteers had successfully resisted the British attempts to suppress the Repub-

Training Camp in Coosan, County Westmeath, 1915 –
Peter Paul Galligan is fifth from the left in the back

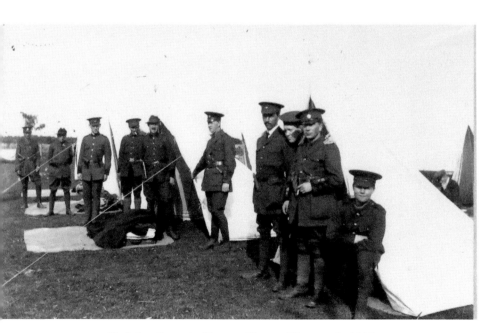

Training Camp in Coosan, County Westmeath, 1915
(L-R): Terence McSwiney, Richard Mulcahy, Michael O'Buachalla,
John Brennan, J.J. Ginger O'Connell, Peter Paul Galligan, Mick Spillane,
Dick Fitzgerald, Larry Lardner, Mick Cremen

Portrait of Peter Paul Galligan

Clockwise from top, Peter Paul Galligan's binoculars, Bible, prison code, baton used during Howth gun running, tunnelling spoon, convict cap and earthenware and mug

Released prisoners, 1917 – Paul Galligan is fifth from the left in the back row

THE
POLICE & GAZETTE

OR
HUE-AND-CRY.

Published by (Authority) for Ireland on every Tuesday and Friday.

REGULATIONS.

☞ All Notices intended for insertion in the "Hue-and-Cry" are to be transmitted, under cover, addressed to the Inspector-General, Royal Irish Constabulary, Dublin Castle, authenticated by a Separate Communication. No Description can be inserted unless an Information shall have been sworn; but it is not necessary to forward the Information to the Inspector-General.

Notices respecting all Felonies and such Misdemeanours as are of an aggravated nature will be inserted.

All Descriptions of persons whose apprehension is sought on a charge of Misdemeanour should be accompanied by a statement that a Warrant has been issued, and by the name of the person in whose hands it is; but the Constabulary should remember that they cannot arrest a person charged with an offence of this nature unless they have the Warrant in their possession when making the arrest.

. Should Irregularities arise in the delivery of the "Hue-and-Cry" it will be necessary to forward one of the covers, or give the number it bears, as without this information the mistake cannot be rectified.

Prison and Police Authorities are particularly requested to be good enough to inform the Inspector-General, Royal Irish Constabulary, Dublin Castle, of the abolition of Gaols, Stations, &c., and of any circumstances rendering the supply of the "Hue-and-Cry" no longer necessary.

Postage should be prepaid at the ordinary rates for printed matter on any copies of this Gazette which may be sent by post within the United Kingdom, except such as are despatched a proper course from a Metropolitan Government Office or from the Publishing Office of the Gazette. Copies sent abroad should be prepaid at the rate of a half-penny for every two ounces.

DUBLIN, TUESDAY, NOVEMBER 11, 1919.

NOTICE

The Composition of the Hue-and-Cry will be arranged for easy reference as follows:—

a. Regulations on top of first page.
b. Apprehensions Sought.
   (1.) Royal Irish Constabulary
   (2.) Dublin Metropolitan Police
   (3.) English Police
   (4.) Scotch Police
c. Animals Stolen.
d. Property Stolen.
e. Apprehensions

APPREHENSIONS SOUGHT.

R.I.C. DISTRICT.

ANTRIM.

ARMAGH.

CARLOW.

CAVAN.

CLARE.

JOHN SCANLON and TIMOTHY HAIER

CORK CITY.

DENIS McNELIS

PATRICK ROCHE

DENIS DESMOND and PATRICK HYDE

CORK, E.R.

Description of JAMES J. MADDEN

Description of THOMAS SCANLON

Description of JEREMIAH SCANLON

Description of CHARLES DUHIG

Paul Galligan features in the Police Gazette,
11 November 1919

Members of the first Dáil – Paul Galligan is standing in the upper right-hand corner

From top, Peter Paul Galligan's train carriage keys,
1916 and War of Independence medals,
and postcard with fellow prisoners Doyle and King

Commandant Peter Paul Galligan

lican administration. Unless the British were willing to maintain such a high level of repression indefinitely, they needed a political settlement with Sinn Féin. A similar dynamic applied in much of Ireland. For this reason, on 11 July 1921 the British and the Irish Republicans agreed to a truce and entered negotiations.

Imprisonment

All of this, of course, happened without Paul Galligan. In Liverpool on 28 October 1920, he did his best to write his father an upbeat letter. 'The weather,' he reported, 'is ideal and if you have the same in Ireland you are lucky.' He was in the prison hospital as a result of his gunshot wound, which had severed the muscles in his arm, but also 'my old enemy, the stomach, which is still making attacks on me and as result I suffer a good deal from a pain in the head'.[50]

From Liverpool, he wrote that 'news from Ireland is scanty, but still it is enough to show what you are suffering'. He was probably referring to the clamour taking place in those days to save the life of Kevin Barry, an 18-year-old IRA Volunteer sentenced to hang for his role in an arms raid in Dublin in which three British soldiers were killed. Barry was executed three days after Galligan wrote that letter to his father, on 1 November 1920. The imprisoned Galligan wrote a poem on Barry's execution that gives a certain insight into how he saw the republican struggle.

Barry is presented as a defiant rebel, unafraid of death, 'a placid smile upon his brow', his 'duty done to Ireland', and a pious figure, to spend 'an eternity with God'.

> Yes, a boy of Eighteen summers
> With defiance in his eye
> He scorns the law of England
> And is now about to die

Yet noble and unmoved he stands
Undaunted to the last
A placid smile upon his brow
While his eyes are upward cast
Soon he will leave his vale of tears
Where sinful man has trod
And exchange it for a happier home
An eternity with God

His duty done to Ireland
He strove to make her free
To burst one more link that binds us
To cursed England o'er the sea
Ah England! Blood stained England
Your crimes surpass the law
Whom you hold up to ridicule

The widow's curse will on you fall
And the child whose father you killed
Will grow up into manhood
With a vow to be fulfilled
To avenge the outrages and wrongs
Committed on his sires
To keep his vow to Erin's Flag
And keep alight her fires.[51]

'Blood stained England', is cast as the oppressor, whose 'crimes surpass the law'. This shows again how Galligan perceived the conflict as one between the legally formed Irish government and the British attempt to suppress it – in the process making a mockery of its own law.

After 12 weeks in Liverpool, Galligan was sent to Lincoln Prison, where the oppression of the British state was very real and obvious. He was recorded as prisoner 1403.[52] As in Dartmoor, there was 'rigid discipline and enforcement of a strict silence', at Lincoln.[53]

The prison experience was more than enough to try the mental strength of the prisoner, but for Paul Galligan it was also mixed with personal tragedy. Not long after his transfer to Lincoln, he received a message from home asking him to apply for parole, as his father was dying.

This came as a great shock to Galligan as his father seemed to have recovered from his stomach illness and his first letters to Belfast and Liverpool prisons had been 'bright and cheery'. It appears that Peter Galligan's health went downhill rapidly after the British raid in which Paul was arrested.

Galligan was denied parole. He commented bitterly to his brother, 'being an Irish criminal I would not be allowed to see my dying father. This was the reply I received an hour before the wire announcing his death.'[54] His father's death and circumstances of it were agonising for Paul Galligan – especially the guilt that none of his family were present at his death bed.

He wrote to his brother: 'Although I was prepared for it, still, it was a great shock to be cut off from all that the world holds dearest, in one blow for he had been a father and a mother to me up to his death. The greater the trouble and the darker the clouds, the more kind he was. As this letter had to pass through indifferent hands I cannot open my heart to you as a brother should to a brother. It would relieve me to be able to tell you my grief and trouble but it cannot be until the prison gates are left behind once more. Poor dad, how I miss you when that day comes. I will miss that bright smile of welcome and joy with which he always had when I returned home. It can never be home to me again. For all that wants to make it a home is gone. Here in my cell at night during those long dreary nights I keep thinking of him, how he must have felt during those last hours with not one of us to say goodbye.'

As during his previous stint in prison, Galligan turned to his religion for comfort: 'Why should I grieve, his last hours were the happiest in his whole life and he died with that pure Irish Catholic prayer on his lips, "Jesus, Mary and Joseph, help me".'[55]

But nevertheless there are signs that towards the end of his prison term in May 1921 he was sinking into a deep depression. What Galligan called, 'the deadly silence of your cell . . . soon leads you to sad and melancholy thoughts. God gave to each and every one of us a brain, the most perfect of all his handwork . . . and a tongue to express . . . but the laws of man say that the tongue must remain silent, the brain dormant.'

'Father's death had its effect for I felt I was going mad and such were the awful fits of depression and despondency, that I would have welcomed madness as a relief. No one holds the greater horror of suicide as I do but looking back on my experience, my horror is turned to pity. For those who don't believe in a hereafter, suicide is a relief from some of the agonies we are called upon to endure. Yes, prison is the hardest place of all to hear that our nearest and dearest is dead. No kind word to cheer you on – no consoling word to give you hope and sympathy.' This state was contributed to by another death, that of his uncle Jonnie: 'I feel his loss almost as much as father's for has he not been more than a father to us all?'

Added to both prison and bereavement was guilt over the future of the family farm. With the estrangement of Jimmy Galligan from his father, and Eugene a priest in Australia, Paul was the last son eligible to inherit the homestead at Drumnalaragh. His father had appealed to him, 'Don't compel me Paul to hand this place over to strangers'. But Galligan 'had made up my mind to a commercial life as I never was in love with farming'.

He was due for release on 11th June and though kept 'as ignorant of Irish events as the man in the moon', he hoped that he could echo one American's reaction to the assassination of Lincoln: 'The American nation lives and there is a just God in heaven.' He feared, however, that he would see on his return home, 'blackened ruins if not worse'.[56]

Back in Ireland on 30 June, Galligan neither went home (where he expected to be arrested and interned again) nor made contact with the Movement for some time. He told his brother that 'a rest was essential' and he was 'in a cosy corner by the coast'.[57] Just 11 days later, a truce agreed between the British and Irish authorities ended hostilities in the War of Independence.

Endnotes

[1.] Paul Galligan to Monsignor Eugene Galligan, 9 October, 1919.

[2.] Summary of the Evidence for the Trial of Peter Paul Galligan of Ballinagh.

[3.] Paul Galligan to Monsignor Eugene Galligan, 9 October, 1919.

[4.] For Police casualties, Richard Abbott, *Police Casualties in Ireland 1919-1921*. For IRA fatalities, IRA monument, the Courthouse, Cavan town. For the informer, Seán Sheridan, Hugh Maguire, Witness Statements BMH.

[5.] For Cork, Peter Hart, *The IRA and its Enemies*, p. 87, For Longford, Marie Coleman, *County Longford and the Irish Revolution*, p. 132-133. For Leitrim, Cormac Ó Suilleabháin, 'Leitrim's Republican Past', *Leitrim Guardian*, no. 79, 2007. For Monaghan, Fearghal McGarry, *Eoin O'Duffy: A Self-Made Hero*, pp. 54, 70-71. The IRA killed 23 in Longford and 21 in Monaghan, but Coleman and McGarry do not list the IRA casualties.

[6.] RIC County Report, Inspector General's report, October-December 1920.

[7.] Seán Sheridan Witness Statement, BMH.

[8.] Paul Galligan to Monsignor Eugene Galligan, 19 December 1919.

[9.] Paul Galligan to Monsignor Eugene Galligan, 15 November 1917.

[10.] Dermot McGonagle, 'Cavan's forgotten contribution to the War of Independence', *History Ireland*, Volume 15, Issue 6.

[11.] Seán Sheridan Witness Statement and Francis Connell Witness Statement, BMH.

[12.] Francis Connell Witness Statement, BMH.

[13.] Witness Statements, Seán Sheridan, Hugh Maguire, Francis Connell, BMH.

[14.] 2012 value, €5,100; Source: Central Bank of Ireland.

[15.] Bernard Brady Witness Statement, BMH.

[16.] Francis Connell Witness Statement, BMH.

[17] Summary of the Evidence for the Trial of Peter Paul Galligan of Ballinagh

[18] Ibid.

[19] Paul Galligan to Monsignor Eugene Galligan, 9 October 1919.

[20] Ibid.

[21] *The Irish Times*, 6/9/1919, p. 8.

[22] Ibid.

[23] Paul Galligan to Monsignor Eugene Galligan, 19 December 1919.

[24] Paul Galligan to Monsignor Eugene Galligan, 9 October 1919.

[25] T. Ryle Dwyer, *Tans, Terror and Troubles: Kerry's Real Fighting Story*, p. 160.

[26] Paul Galligan to Monsignor Eugene Galligan, 20 April 1920.

[27] Seamus MacDiarmada Witness Statement, BMH.

[28] Seán Sheridan and Hugh Maguire Witness Statements, BMH.

[29] Hugh Maguire Witness Statement BMH.

[30] Seán Sheridan Witness Statement BMH.

[31] Ibid.

[32] Seamus MacDiarmada Witness Statement, BMH.

[33] Ibid.

[34] Peter Galligan to Monsignor Eugene Galligan, 9 September 1920.

[35] Ibid.

[36] *Anglo Celt,* 11/09/1920, p. 1.

[37] Seamus MacDiarmada Witness Statement, BMH

[38] County Inspector's Report, 1919, CO 904/109, The National Archives, Kew, Richmond, Surrey, TW9 4DU, England.

[39] Hugh Maguire Witness Statement, BMH.

[40] Francis Connell Witness Statement, BMH.

[41] Seán Sheridan, Seamus McKenna and Seamus MacDiarmada, Witness Statements, BMH.

[42] Cavan IRA memorial.

[43] Seamus McKenna Witness Statement, BMH.

44. Ibid.

45. James Cahill Witness Statement, BMH.

46. Hugh Maguire Witness Statement, BMH.

47. HC Deb 16 June 1921 vol 143 cc571-4. http://hansard. millbanksystems.com/commons/1921/jun/16/murders

48. T. C. Maguire, N.T, *Breifne Journal of Cumann Seánchais Bhreifne* (Breifne Historical Society) Volume IV No 14 (1971).

49. Francis Connell Witness Statement, BMH.

50. Paul to Peter Galligan, 28 October 1920.

51. Peter Paul Galligan Papers [P25], Archives Department, UCD, Dublin 4.

52. See Appendix II for the full Lincoln prison record.

53. Paul Galligan to Monsignor Eugene Galligan, 29 May 1921.

54. Paul Galligan to Monsignor Eugene Galligan, 2 March 1921.

55. Ibid.

56. Paul Galligan to Monsignor Eugene Galligan, 29 May 1921.

57. Paul Galligan to Monsignor Eugene Galligan, 30 June 1921.

Chapter 7

Truce, Treaty and Civil War, 1921-22

The truce of 11 July, 1921 ended open hostilities between the British forces and the IRA and for roughly a year, Ireland had a period of fitful peace. In December 1921, the Anglo Irish Treaty was signed – disestablishing the Republic declared in 1919 replacing it with the Irish Free State, a self-governing dominion of the British Empire. A separate entity, Northern Ireland, which was first created in mid-1920, was confirmed under the Treaty. It was to remain part of the United Kingdom, with some powers of self-government.

The Free State was a major advance for Irish nationalists compared to the terms offered in Home Rule. An Irish government would have full sovereign control over its territory. It would have control over taxation and fiscal policies. The British Army would leave its territory and be replaced by independent Irish armed forces. The RIC would be disbanded and replaced by a native police force.

On the other hand, as far as republicans were concerned, there were major drawbacks to the Treaty settlement. They had established, as they saw it, an independent Irish Republic. Now they were asked to accept voluntarily the dissolution of that Republic and to accept – albeit in largely symbolic terms – the sovereignty of the British monarch over Ireland. TDs elected to the new Dáil would have to swear an Oath of Allegiance to the King. The British also retained three strategic naval bases on the Free State's territory and it was also not until the Statute of Westminster in 1931 that the British Parliament gave up the right to legislate for Ireland.

The issue of partition was also objectionable to many nationalists but did not figure so prominently in the debates. For one thing, many thought Northern Ireland was not viable in the long term, and under the Treaty it could opt in to the Free State in December 1922. Paul Galligan certainly seems to have expected it do so. In a letter of June 1921, he wrote: 'The humblest Unionist sees that his parliament is a fiasco – worse is a financial bankrupt and a new feeling is sweeping over Ulster and it is that if Ulster must be prosperous there must be only one parliament.'[1] Under the Treaty a Border Commission was established to redraw the border and was expected to cede those parts of Northern Ireland with Catholic, nationalist majorities to the Free State. Michael Collins at the head of the Free State's Provisional Government and also commander in chief of its Army, remained committed in secret to undermining the northern state by force. There was some attempt to do this in early 1922.

The Treaty caused a bitter split between those prepared to accept the compromise of the Treaty and those who held out for the Republic. By July 1922, a little under a year after the truce, the IRA had split into two hostile factions and civil war had broken out between pro and anti-Treaty factions. The Civil War dragged on until April 1923, when the Free State government by wholesale arrests and selective executions, ground down the anti-Treaty guerrillas, who called a ceasefire and dumped their arms.

Unlike the Easter Rising of 1916 or the War of Independence of 1919-1921, the Civil War was not something that participants liked to remember or to celebrate. Todd Andrews, an anti-Treaty IRA fighter, later wrote of it, 'in civil war there is no glory, no monuments to victory or the victors, only to the dead'.[2]

Perhaps for this reason, it is much more difficult to pin down the part that Paul Galligan played in the events after the truce of 1921. His statement to the Bureau of Military History ends in 1917 and his personal correspondence does not go beyond mid-1921. The Witness Statements by his comrades, with the very odd exception, likewise stop in 1921.

Galligan was clearly torn over the Treaty split. He voted for the Treaty as a TD in January 1922 but also voted for Éamon de Valera as President, the man who led political opposition to the Treaty. He retired his Dáil seat before the election of June 1922 and largely retired from politics thereafter. In the Civil War itself, he seems to have remained neutral – giving some verbal support to the anti-Treaty IRA in private but playing no part in the actual fighting.

The Truce Period

On the 24 May 1921, there were elections to the British-created Parliaments of Northern and Southern Ireland. Southern Ireland was short-lived parliament in the 26 counties created under the 1920 Government of Ireland Act with Home Rule powers. It was boycotted by Sinn Féin who nevertheless won 124 seats (all unopposed) out of 128 – the remaining four were taken by unionist representatives for Trinity College, also uncontested.

Paul Galligan, though still imprisoned, was re-elected, unopposed, as Sinn Féin, MP for Cavan along with Arthur Griffith and Seán Milroy. By the time Dáil Éireann, which had been suppressed during the War of Independence, re-convened on 16 August 1921, Galligan was again at liberty and attended.

He wrote to his brother just after his return to Ireland that he needed a rest and had secluded himself at some spot near the coast, but it was not long before he was back in Cavan and trying to use the cessation of hostilities to reorganise the Volunteers and the Sinn Féin administration there.

British Intelligence, which regarded Galligan as 'the prime mover and Chief Organiser of the Cavan Brigade; responsible for arming the IRA in Cavan [and] one of the most dangerous men in the Rebel Movement', kept a close eye on his activities. On 2 August, about a month after his return to Ireland he again

became Commandant of the Cavan Brigade. He ran IRA training camps at Glencirrick Castle, Carrigallen, County Leitrim
in September and at Crosskeys in October. Also in that month
he reviewed 200 IRA Volunteers in his native Ballinagh.[3]

It was not obvious, in the autumn of 1921, that the Truce
was a permanent end to the fighting. The Republican Army
tried to use the respite to ensure it would be in a much stronger
situation to take on British forces if fighting resumed. The IRA
had been massively expanded, from about 3,000 fighters up to
72,000 by early 1922. Training camps had sprung up around
the country and mass demonstrations had been performed for
the benefit of the world's press.[4]

Between July and October 1921, there were several exchange of letters between Paul Galligan and Austin Stack,
Minister of Home Affairs, about the operation of the Republican courts. The courts had been at the heart of the revolution,
in effect enabling the Republicans to replace British law with
their own. In the 'reign of terror', as Republicans described
the conflict of 1919-21, the courts had been persecuted and
driven underground. During the Truce, the Republican government was determined to ensure that the Republican courts
continued to operate and they introduced an emergency plan
to re-organise the courts. This would lessen the chance of 'the
enemy' preventing them from functioning should hostilities
resume.

Stack wrote to Galligan on 26 September: 'I am afraid the
importance of putting the court machinery in perfect working order is not fully appreciated in your constituency. While
not wishing to depreciate the importance of not using every
opportunity for perfecting the training of the army, I think it
is rather unfortunate that all the important work of Court Organisation should be allowed to suffer or remain in abeyance
for this purpose.'[5]

Galligan served as the Presiding Judge at a Sinn Féin court
at Gowna 13 August 1921 but initially the reorganisation of
the courts seems not to have been a priority for him. Rather,
he appears to have been focussed on using the Truce period

to retrain and reorganise his Battalion. However, by October 1921, Galligan had begun to reorganise the Cavan courts. British Intelligence reported that he arbitrated at a Sinn Féin court at Templeport Hall on 11 October.[6]

The Treaty

The Treaty was signed on 5 December 1921.[7] In a famous exchange, F.E. Smith, Earl Birkenhead, one of the British negotiators, told Michael Collins who had headed the Irish team, 'I may have signed my political death warrant'. 'I may have signed my actual death warrant,' Collins replied.[8] Nine months later he was dead, killed by his former IRA comrades in an ambush in his native Cork.

The Irish team brought back an already-signed Treaty to the Dáil for them to approve or reject, but with the threat of war looming should they take the latter option. Éamon de Valera was furious that the negotiators had signed the deal without first consulting him or his cabinet.[9] After a stormy debate, the Dáil narrowly passed the Treaty on 7 January 1922, by 64 votes to 57. Paul Galligan did not speak in the debate but voted for the Treaty.

On the face of it, Galligan's acceptance of the Treaty seems surprising. Back in 1910, on joining the IRB, he had sworn to 'do my utmost to establish the independence of Ireland, and that I will bear true allegiance to the Supreme Council of the Irish Republican Brotherhood and the Government of the Irish Republic'. He had never accepted the prospect of Home Rule or anything less than a Republic in the years leading up to the Treaty. So why did he accept the compromise of 1922?

One clue may be in the second part of his IRB oath, to 'implicitly obey the constitution of the Irish Republican Brotherhood and all my superior officers and that I will preserve inviolable the secrets of the organisation'. The IRB was now headed by Michael Collins, who saw the Treaty as a 'stepping stone' or tactical step on the road to full independence. He and Richard Mulcahy used the organisation to help pass the

Treaty. Cathal Brugha, the anti-Treaty leader, alleged that up to 40 TDs voted for the Treaty as result of their IRB affiliation.[10]

Seamus McKenna, the Belfast IRA man, captured at Lapinduff in Cavan in May 1921, went pro-Treaty and found himself fighting with the Free State Army in the Civil War as a result of the advice of his IRB centre, Pat Casey. He later regretted this choice and pondered, 'I am sure that many other IRB men accepted that ill-fated Treaty on the advice of their officers in that organisation'.[11]

But perhaps there is no need to look for conspiracies or the hidden hand of secret organisations as reasons for Galligan's vote. Another powerful factor in his decision was that public opinion in Cavan was overwhelmingly pro-Treaty. Galligan received a host of telegrams and letters from public bodies and parish councils in Cavan in the weeks leading up to the vote on the Treaty urging him to ratify it.

The Cavan town Urban District Council, for example, wrote of its 'high appreciation of the terms of the Treaty' and urged all TDs 'for the sake of our country to bury their differences and stand with Arthur Griffith and Seán McKeon [MacEoin] for the ratification of the Treaty'.[12] The Swanlibar Sinn Féin Club 'trusts that the Treaty shall lead to the establishment of a Republic at no distant date' and urged ratification, 'to prevent the appalling consequences of split'. The Belturbet District Council thought that '99 per cent of the people call for Ratification'. Seamus MacDiarmada, the Cavan IRA intelligence officer remembered: 'Every public body in Cavan urged its acceptance, members who had not attended in years turned up to support it. My proposition against it [the Treaty] caused much the same reaction as an atomic blast would today [1952] in Cavan town – [the council] voting 15 for 3 against.'[13]

It would have been difficult in these circumstances for Galligan to vote against the wishes of his constituents. It was clear that, for most people, the Treaty was a good enough start to national self-determination, and certainly very few wanted a return to hostilities with the British which might ensue if the Treaty was rejected. And it is also possible that Galligan himself thought the Treaty was indeed an acceptable 'stepping stone' to independence. British intelligence reported that, just after the Treaty's signing, he 'made an important speech in West Cavan in favour of [the] Treaty'.[14]

On 9 January, President Éamon de Valera offered his resignation to the Dáil. During this debate, a motion was proposed that Éamon de Valera should be re-elected President of Dáil Éireann. The motion was narrowly rejected by 60 votes to 58 votes. The intensity of the feelings unleashed by the Treaty debate may be glimpsed in the following exchange, as the anti-Treaty TDs, in protest at the ratification of the Treaty and the replacement of de Valera as President, left the House:

> **Mr. de Valera:** *As a protest against the election as President of the Irish Republic of the Chairman of the Delegation, who is bound by the Treaty conditions to set up a State which is to subvert the Republic, and who, in the interim period, instead of using the office as it should be used – to support the Republic – will, of necessity, have to be taking action which will tend to its destruction, I, while this vote is being taken, as one, am going to leave the House.*
>
> **Mr. Collins:** *Deserters all! We will now call on the Irish people to rally to us. Deserters all!*
>
> **Mr. Ceannt:** *Up the Republic!*
>
> **Mr. Collins:** *Deserters all to the Irish nation in her hour of trial. We will stand by her.*
>
> **Madame Markievicz:** *Oath breakers and cowards.*
>
> **Mr. Collins:** *Foreigners – Americans – English.*[15]
>
> **Madame Markievicz:** *Lloyd Georgeites.*

Galligan voted in favour of keeping de Valera as President. Whatever his reasons for voting for the Treaty, his admiration for 'The Chief' dated back to their time at Dartmoor Prison, when de Valera had been the leader capable of organising resistance among the Volunteers to the brutal prison system.

Galligan was only one of two deputies that voted in favour of the Treaty but also voted in favour of the re-election of Éamon de Valera as President. The other deputy was Robert Barton who was elected unopposed as the Sinn Féin member for West Wicklow. He was appointed Minister for Agriculture and was one of the Irish delegates, along with his cousin (Erskine Childers), to travel to London for the Anglo-Irish Treaty negotiations. He reluctantly signed the Treaty on 6 December 1921, defending it 'as the lesser of two outrages forced upon me and between which I had to choose'.

Despite signing and voting for the Treaty, in the June 1922 general elections, Barton was re-elected as the Anti-Treaty Sinn Féin member for Kildare Wicklow. It could be that Galligan had a similar disposition and voted in favour of the Treaty as the better between two evils.

The Descent into Civil War

The outbreak of the Irish Civil War on 28 June 1922 was preceded by six tortuous months, in which both Sinn Féin and the IRA split into antagonistic factions. Paul Galligan seems not to have taken either side, but there are indications that he grew increasingly disillusioned with the pro-Treaty side as 1922 went on.

On the appointment of Patrick Hogan as Minister of Agriculture on 28 February, Paul Galligan voted against the government and against the appointment. The motion was carried by 56 votes to 50 against. Hogan, along with Kevin O'Higgins, was the type of pro-Treatyite most disliked by Republicans – he had no military record, disliked the IRB and was indifferent to cultural nationalism. To people with backgrounds like Galligan's Hogan, despite having been elected for Sinn Féin, must have looked more like the old constitutional nationalists of the IPP than a real Republican.[16]

On 26 March 1922, the Anti-Treaty IRA officers held an Army Convention in the Mansion House in Dublin, in which they repudiated the right of the Dáil to abolish the Republic. They went on to elect their own 16 man Army Executive, led by Rory O'Connor, who had been the IRA's Head of Engineering, and Liam Mellows, who had led the Easter Rising in Galway back in 1916.[17]

Fighting almost broke out in Limerick between pro- and anti-Treaty forces over who would occupy the barracks vacated there by the British. On 14 April, 200 anti-Treaty IRA men under Rory O'Connor occupied the Four Courts in Dublin in defiance of the Free State's Provisional government.

In Paul Galligan's native Cavan, the British garrison left Cavan barracks on 4 March 1922, handing over to the troops of the new Irish Free State, represented at the handover ceremony by Commandant Michael Gilheaney. There had already been a controversy in the County between pro and anti-Treaty elements. In the Dáil on 2 March, Galligan raised the question of the arrest of several IRA men in Cavan by pro-Treaty troops.

Paul Galligan: *(a) When may officers and men of No. 1 Battalion W. Cavan Brigade arrested on Friday 13 January and detained for 5 days, expect to be court-martialled? (b) By whose authority did Brig. Woods, commanding the West Cavan Brigade, raid the homes of 10 families in the parish of Templeport on the 14 January and what is the name of the Justice who signed the warrant authorising him to search those houses?*

He didn't receive a satisfactory answer.

The Minister of Defence, Mr. Mulcahy: *The information is not available at the moment. It may take three or four days to procure. If the Dáil is in Session the information will be passed direct to the Deputy asking the question.*

In June 1922, just before the Free State's first General Election, Paul Galligan retired his seat and from active politics. Perhaps he was distressed by the increasingly acrimonious split between former comrades, or perhaps he was simply tired of the struggle and wanted to settle down with his new wife Mollie – the two were married in the summer of 1922.

In the election of June 1922, pro-Treaty Sinn Féin won, with 239,193 votes to 133,864 for anti-Treaty Sinn Féin. A further 247,226 people voted for other parties, all of whom supported the Treaty.[18] Just ten days later, Civil War broke out when Michael Collins' pro-Treaty troops opened fire on the anti-Treaty IRA in the Four Courts in Dublin. Collins had been trying for several months to re-unite the two factions, but after the assassination of a British general, Henry Wilson, by two IRA men in London, Winston Churchill delivered him an ultimatum to move against the anti-Treaty forces or the British themselves would do it. Collins would justifiably claim that he had the democratic backing of the Irish people and could not tolerate two rival armies in the country. On the other hand, the anti-Treaty forces, led by Liam Lynch, argued that they had never intended to take power by force, but were simply trying to preserve the Republic in defiance of British pressure by keeping the Republican Army in existence.[19]

For nine months, from 28 June 1922 until 30 April 1923, the two sides, both of whom believed they represented the wishes of the people and were the victims of the other's aggression, would wage civil war.

Paul Galligan and the Civil War

Paul Galligan's role in the Civil War is murky and can only be glimpsed through the captured correspondence of Ernie O'Malley, head of the anti-Treaty IRA's 1st Eastern Division. It appears as if, not long after the outbreak of fighting, Galligan gave some indication to the anti-Treaty, or Republican, side, that he would join them.

On 14 July, 1922, O'Malley wrote to Oscar Traynor, leader of the anti-Treaty IRA Dublin Brigade: 'Please instruct Joe Griffin to place a good officer in charge of communications and see that he gets in touch with the Brigades of the 1st Eastern, the Dundalk Brigades, O'Meighan of the 5 Northern and the Cavan Brigade under Paul Galligan. I would require to meet these officers somewhere near Dublin so that outlook and operations could be unified.'[20]

Early in July, there was some fighting in Cavan. Ballyjamesduff barracks was attacked and taken by the anti-Treatyites, though O'Malley complained that, 'as far as I could gather a considerable amount of rifle ammunition was used (unnecessarily) in the attack on the barracks'.[21] On 26 July, the Cavan IRA memorial records that 'Staff Capt. Edward P. Boylan, Corratober, Cavan. Cavan Brigade [anti-Treaty] died of wounds received in action' – according to O'Malley's papers he was shot trying to escape from Cavan barracks.[22]

A report in August 1922 shows that there were about 80-100 anti-Treaty IRA fighters active in West Cavan, but equipped with only 12 rifles and 20 handguns. There were 30 Free State troops in Belturbet barracks and parties of five to six in several former RIC barracks, including ten in Ballinagh who were evacuated on 31 August. The anti-Treaty leadership concluded that 'the enemy there are very undisciplined and untrained; the whole Brigade is weakly held', but their own men were, 'very disorganised' as result of many arrests of the senior officers there. Worse, 'the people are for the most part hostile'.[23]

Ernie O'Malley informed his superiors on the 3 September that he was 'meeting a man from the West Cavan area tonight' in Dublin. This seems to have been Paul Galligan. Frank Aiken, who was put in charge of the anti-Treaty units in the border area, reported of West Cavan, 'Paul Galligan was OC of this Bde but had not been in it for two months'.[24] O'Malley relayed the information to Liam Lynch, the IRA chief of Staff: 'OC of the West Cavan Bde is Paul Galligan; he has not left Dublin yet. There are no other efficient officers for that area.' Lynch replied: 'Who is this OC West Cavan? Hurry him off out of Dublin to work the area.'[25]

On 1 October, 1922, Lynch wrote in irritation to O'Malley: 'If OC West Cavan does not leave Town at once, he should be dismissed. He is of no use where he is.' In fact, Frank Aiken had already lost patience and appointed Patrick Smith as officer commanding the Cavan Brigade, which he created by an amalgamation of East and West Cavan units. Patrick Smith was arrested by Free State troops in October.[26] There are no more records of the part Galligan played, if any, in the Civil War, as Ernie O'Malley was arrested and his papers seized after a shootout at his safe house at Ailesbury Road, Dublin in early November.

It is difficult to know what to make of this fragmentary evidence. It could be that Paul Galligan was in sympathy with the anti-Treaty side but in the end could not stomach fighting against his former comrades. Or it could be that he made some non-committal noises to O'Malley which O'Malley misinterpreted. In the final analysis, we just do not know.

The Civil War in Cavan

In Cavan, most of the people were pro-Treaty as were some of the most active pre-truce IRA Volunteers such as James Cahill and Bernard Brady, who both joined the Free State's National Army.[27] By late 1922, although the county was 'weakly held' by pro-Treaty troops, the anti-Treaty forces there did not pose a major threat. In September 1922 the first detachment of the new, unarmed, police force, An Garda Siochána, took up residence in Cavan town – a sign that the area was considered one of the more secure in the country.

What actions there were in the County tended to be raids from anti-Treaty columns based in Arigna Mountains in Leitrim. On 13 November 1922, one civilian, James Martin, was shot dead by armed raiders from Leitrim at his home at Drumcar, Cavan, and on 10 December 1922 there was a 'large scale raid' on Black Lion, Cavan, by 60 guerrillas, who took supplies from the shops, and kidnapped a Free State supporter, Doctor Hamilton. No Free State troops were in the area.[28]

On 6 January 1923 an anti-Treaty IRA Volunteer from Roscommon, Michael Cull, was killed in a skirmish with Free State troops during a raid on Ballyconnell, County Cavan. A month later, apparently in reprisal, what the National Army described as 'a party of about 50 Irregulars [anti-Treaty IRA], fully armed and with three machine guns, entered Ballyconnell'. In the town, they shot dead two men, William Ryan and John McGrath, and wounded a third. Food was taken from the town's shops and a car dealership blown up and burned. Free State troops based at Belturbet barracks and Cavan town pursued the guerrillas back to the Arigna Mountains, but 'failed to get in touch with them'.[29]

In February and March 1923, several thousand Free State troops mounted an extensive sweep of the Arigna area, west of Cavan, in search of this column, finally tracking it down and arresting its leader, Ned Boffin, on 25 March 1923.[30]

As in many other parts of the country, by the time Frank Aiken (who became IRA Chief of Staff in April 1923 after the death in action of Liam Lynch) called a ceasefire and ordered his men to 'dump arms' on 30 May, the Civil War in Cavan had already effectively ended in victory for the pro-Treaty side.

The final two deaths connected with the conflict in Cavan were those of anti-Treaty IRA Volunteers, Andy O'Sullivan, a Cavan man attached to the Cork Brigade, and Thomas Fitzpatrick of the Cavan Brigade, who died on hunger strike in Free State internment camps in November 1923 and February 1924 respectively.[31]

Whereas in 1922 three pro-Treaty candidates were elected in Cavan, in the 1923 election, pro-Treaty candidate Seán Milroy was re-elected but so too was the Republican candidate Patrick Smith (who was imprisoned at the time), along with Farmers' Party candidate Patrick Baxter (who topped the poll) and an independent, John Cole. The election of two candidates not affiliated with either wing of the nationalist movement is a clear sign that the population at large was weary with the struggle and wanted a return to normal life. The sharp decline in the pro-Treaty vote may well have been a reaction against the harsh suppression of the anti-Treaty guerrillas in the Civil War.[32]

The Civil War was a sad and largely futile end to the Irish revolution. Dismay at the internecine fighting between his former comrades probably hastened Paul Galligan's exit from politics and ended his own personal career as a revolutionary.

Endnotes

1. Paul Galligan to Monsignor Eugene Galligan, 30 June 1921.

2. Todd Andrews, *Dublin Made Me*, p. 254.

3. Dublin Castle File No. 88, GALLIGAN, Peter Paul, WO 35/207, The National Archives, Kew, Richmond, Surrey, TW9 4DU, England.

4. Michael Hopkinson, *Green Against Green: The Irish Civil War*, p. 16.

5. Peter Paul Galligan Collection [CD 105], Military Archives, Cathal Brugha Barracks, Dublin 6.

6. Peter Paul Galligan Dublin Castle File, no 88.

7. Michael Hopkinson, *Green Against Green: The Irish Civil War*, p. 30-32.

8. Tim Pat Coogan, *Michael Collins*, p. 276.

9. John Regan, *The Irish Counter Revolution*, p. 10.

10. Michael Hopkinson, *Green Against Green: The Irish Civil War*, p. 44-45.

11. Seamus McKenna Witness Statement, BMH.

12. Galligan papers, UCD archives.

13. Seamus MacDiarmada Witness Statement, BMH.

14. Galligan Dublin Castle File.

15. This was a disparaging reference to Éamon de Valera, who had been born in New York, and Erskine Childers, who was born in London.

16. John Regan, *The Irish Counter Revolution*, p. 89.

17. Michael Hopkinson, *Green Against Green: The Irish Civil War*, p. 67.

18. Paul V Walsh, *The Irish Civil War – A study of the Conventional Phase*.

19. Michael Hopkinson, *Green Against Green: The Irish Civil War*, p. 112-116.

20. Cormac KH O'Malley and Anne Dolan (eds.), *No Surrenders Here! The Civil War Papers of Ernie O'Malley*, p. 53.

21. O'Malley, Dolan, pp. 141-142.

22. IRA memorial Cavan Courthouse, O'Malley, Dolan, p. 215.

23. Cormac KH O'Malley and Anne Dolan, pp. 141-142, 186.

[24.] Ibid., p. 186.

[25.] Ibid., p. 212.

[26.] Ibid., p. 239.

[27.] James Cahill and Bernard Brady Witness Statements, BMH.

[28.] *New York Times*, 15/12/1922.

[29.] Dáil debates, 8 February 1923.

[30.] Hopkinson, *Green Against Green: The Irish Civil War*, pp. 243-244.

[31.] Cavan IRA memorial, Cavan Courthouse.

[32.] For the results of these elections in Cavan see Elections Ireland at http://electionsireland.org/result.cfm?election=1923&cons=36 and http://electionsireland.org/result.cfm?election=1922&cons=36

Epilogue

Paul Galligan resigned from Dáil Éireann in June 1922 and took no further active part in politics. He had written in May 1921 that he intended to set up a business and he did indeed go on to become a successful businessman. He was founder and Managing Director of Cumberland Warehouse Ltd. and Galligan's Ltd. in Henry Street, Dublin.

He had suffered severely during the revolutionary period, living on the run, serving four prison sentences in the most brutal of conditions and being shot and badly injured. But his post-revolutionary life was good to him. He lived in a spacious house in what was then a semi-rural suburb of Dublin at Churchtown.

He was also appointed a director of the *Irish Press* – the pro-Fianna Fáil newspaper set up by Éamon de Valera. This seems to indicate quite strongly that his gut sympathies lay with the anti-Treaty side of the Civil War split.

He married Mollie Coyle in 1922 and had five sons and two daughters: Eugene, Peter, Máirín, Liam, Sarah, Brendan and Colm.

The ending of the Irish revolution in civil war and partition left a great many nationalist activists bitterly disillusioned. Others were dismayed that problems they had assumed would go away once the British were removed, such as emigration and unemployment, continued as before in an independent Ireland. Many anti-Treatyites had great difficulty accepting the Free State as the rightful inheritor of the revolution. It was not until de Valera came to power in 1932, and introduced a new constitution in 1937, that most of them were reconciled to the Irish state.

We have no real indication of where Paul Galligan stood on these debates. He rarely spoke about his young life as a revolutionary, even to his family. But whatever the shortcomings of independence, there is no reason to think that he was not proud of his role in winning Irish freedom. His witness statement, given in 1948 to the Bureau of Military History, on his role in the Easter Rising certainly shows no regrets.

In November 1966, Paul Galligan was honoured at a ceremony in Enniscorthy for the part he played in the fight for Irish freedom. He received an illuminated scroll from the then President of Ireland, Éamon de Valera. A month later, on 15 December, Paul Galligan died at his home in Churchtown, Dublin.

There was a large attendance from political, religious and business circles at his funeral. Full military honours were recorded and among the attendance were President Éamon de Valera, Seán Lemass and Lieutenant General Seán MacEoin. The Taoiseach, Jack Lynch, was represented by his private secretary. Paul Galligan was buried in Deansgrange Cemetery, County Dublin.

Appendix I

Letter Addressed to the President and Congress of the United States

To the President and Congress of the United States.
Dublin, June 18, 1917.

Gentlemen,

We, the undersigned, who have been held in English prisons, and have been dragged from dungeon to dungeon, in heavy chains, cut off since Easter Week, 1916, from all intercourse with the outside world, have just had an opportunity of seeing the printed text of the message of the United States of America to the Provisional Government of Russia.

We see that the President accepts as the aim of both countries 'the carrying of the present struggle for the freedom of all peoples to a successful consummation.' We also see that the object of President Wilson's own Government is 'the liberation of peoples everywhere from the aggressions of autocratic force.' 'We are fighting,' writes the President to the Government of Russia, 'for the liberty, self-government and undictated development of all peoples, and every feature of the settlement that concludes this war must be conceived and executed for that purpose. Wrongs must first be righted and then adequate safeguards must be created to prevent their being committed again. Remedies must be found as well as statements of principle that will have a pleasing and sonorous sound.' No people must be forced under a sovereignty under which it does not wish to live.'

We trust that such remedies – in preference to any governmental professions whatsoever - will be held to include the right of each people, not merely to rely on other peoples to support their claim to national liberty, but what the Governments and peoples of other nations will, we trust, regard as even more sacred the right of each people to defend itself against external aggression, external interference and external control. It is this particular right that we claim for the Irish people, and not content with statements of principle, though these themselves may be made a pretext for our oppression, we are engaged and mean to engage ourselves in the practical means for establishing this right.

Without awaiting the issue of the war or the settlement that may conclude the war, we ask the Government of the United States of America, and the Governments of the free peoples of the world, to take immediate measures to inform themselves accurately and on the spot about the extent of liberty or attempted repression which we may encounter.

We, the undersigned, are officers (just released from English prisons) of forces formed independently in Ireland to secure the complete liberation of the Irish Nation.

Edward de Valera	*John R. Etchingham*	*Richard Coleman*
Eoin MacNeill	*Richard F. King*	*George Irvine*
Denis O'Callaghan	*John Irvine*	*Con. Collins*
James Lawless	*Richard Hayes*	*Austin Stack*
Robert Brennan	*James Doyle*	*John McGarry*
M. D. de Lacy	*Peter Galligan*	*James J. Walsh*
Finian Lynch	*Thomas Ashe*	*Francis Thornton*
Francis Fahy	*Jeremiah C. Lynch*	*Frank Lawless*
Thomas Hunter	*T. Desmond Fitzgerald*	

Appendix II

Lincoln Prison Records

Records in Lincoln Prison have the following entries for Paul Galligan:

Register Number: 1403
Offence: Defence of Realm (3 charges)
Education: 2 (scoring is on a rating of 0 to 3)
Sentence: 1 Year HL
Age, Height and Colour of Hair: 29 / 5.9 / L Brn
Trade or Occupation: Farmer
Religion and Birth Place: RC Ireland
Previous Convictions: Yes
Date of Discharge / On Expiration of Sentence: 6.8.21
Date of Discharge / On Remission: 11.6.21
Remarks: Lost Marks – remission altered by 4 days

Appendix III

Dublin Castle File

The following is a direct transcription of Dublin Castle File
No. 88 held by the British authorities on Peter Paul Galligan:

GALLIGAN, Peter Paul
Galligan. Peter. Paul. Ballinagh, Co. Cavan.
Drumlaragh, Gossdoney, Co. Cavan
A2/2169

Age,
Occupation, Drapers' Assistant.
ELECTED SINN FÉIN M.P. FOR CO. CAVAN, MAY 1921
Prior to May 1921 Election, was a member of Agricultural
Committee, Dáil Éireann.
Provincial Representative, I.R.A. Executive, (1921).

Commandant, Cavan Brigade, I.R.A.

Commandant, Ballanagh Battalion, Cavan Brigade, I.R.A. (O.
of B.)

A native of Drumlaragh, Crossdoney, Co. Cavan.

Is the prime mover and Chief Organiser of the Cavan Brigade;
and responsible for arming the I.R.A. in Cavan.

Considered one of the most dangerous men in the Rebel Movement.

As a Captain in the Irish Volunteers took part in the Rebellion of 1916 at Enniscorthy, Co. Wexford.

Was arrested and sentenced to death, but sentence afterwards commuted to 5 years penal servitude.

Released at the General Amnesty in June 1917.

Attended Sinn Féin Convention in Dublin, October 1917.

Elected T.D. for West Cavan at the General Election in December 1918.

Addressed a number of Sinn Féin Meetings and promised the Irish Volunteers that he would provide them with rifles.

One of those who signed the Petition to President Wilson by the Irish Volunteers.

Arrested 8 July 1918 and deported. Released 11 March 1919.

Again arrested, and tried by court martial at Belfast on 25 July 1919 for illegal drilling.

Sentenced to 12 months imprisonment with hard labour.

Went on 'Hunger Strike' and was released under the 'Temporary Release for Ill-health Act' in September 1919, but failed to report back.

Re-arrested in September 1920, sent back to prison and recommended for internment on expiration of sentence.

Released from Prison on 21 July 1921.

ACTIVITIES SINCE THE TRUCE

Reported to have again become Commandant (Brigade), 2-8-21. ('O' I.F.99/5/7).

Presiding Judge at a Sinn Féin Court at Gowna 13th August 1921.

Commandant I.R.A. Camp, Glencirrick Castle, Carrigallen, Co. Leitrim. (D.W. 1. 15-9-21).

Arbitrated at a Sinn Féin Court at Templeport Hall on 11-10-21.

Reported to be in Camp at Crosskeys which was established on the 8th inst. (IX/0235 dated 16-10-21).

Believed to be in charge of the West Cavan Boycott Committee. (IX/0226 dated 15-10-21).

Reviewed about 200 of the I.R.A. on 23 October 1921 near Ballinagh. (IX/0427).

Made an important speech in West Cavan in favour of Treaty. (IX/0861 22-12-21).

Voted in favour of ratification of the Treaty on Saturday, 7 January 1922.

Subsequently voted for De Valera as 'President of the Irish Republic'. (Ex. 'Irish Independent' dated 30.5.22.)

Retired. June 1922. Replaced by W.L. Cole. (119)

Appendix IV

Votes For and Against the Treaty, 7 January 1922

FOR:

Mícheál O Coileáin
Art O Gríobhtha
Seán Mac Giolla Ríogh
Pól O Geallagáin
Liam T. Mac Cosgaír
Gearóid O Súileabháin
Pádraig O Braonáin
Seán O Lidia
Seán O hAodha
Pádraig O Caoimh
Seán Mac Héil
Seosamh Mac Suibhne
Peadar S. Mac an Bháird
Dr. S. Mac Fhionnlaoigh
P.S. Mac Ualghairg
Próinsias Laighléis
S. Ghabháin Uí Dhubhthaigh
Deasmhumhain Mac Gearailt
Seumas Mac Doirim
Seumas O Duibhir
Pádraic O Máille
Seoirse Mac Niocaill

P.S. O hOgáin
An t-Oll. S. O Faoilleacháin
Piaras Béaslaí
Fionán O Loingsigh
S. O Cruadhlaoich
Riobárd Bartún
Criostóir O Broin
Seumas O Dóláin
Aindriú O Láimhín
Tomás Mac Artúir
Dr. Pádraig Mac Artáin
Caoimhghín O hUigín
Seosamh O Loingsigh
Próinsias Bulfin
Dr. Risteárd O hAodha
Liam O hAodha
Seosamh Mac Aonghusa
Seán Mac Eoin
Lorcán O Roibín
Eamon O Dúgáin
Peadar O hAodha
Seumas O Murchadha
Saerbhreathach Mac Cionaith

Seosamh Mac Giolla Bhrighde
Liam Mac Sioghuird
Domhnall O Ruairc
Earnán de Blaghd
Eoin O Dubhthaigh
Alasdar Mac Cába
Tomás O Domhnaill
Seumas de Búrea
Dr. V. de Faoite
Risteárd Mac Fheorais
Seán Mac Gadhra
Mícheál Mac Stáin
Risteárd O Maolchatha
Seosamh Mag Craith
Pilib Mac Cosgair
Domhnall Mac Cárthaigh
Liam de Róiste
Seumas Breathnach
Mícheál O hAodha

AGAINST:
Seumas O Lonnáin
Eamon Aidhleart
Eamon de Valera
Brian O hUigín
Seán Mac Suibhne
Seán O Maoláin
Domhnall O Corcora
Seán O Nualláin
Tomás O Fiadhchara
Seumas Mac Gearailt
Dáithí Ceannt
Seosamh O Dochartaigh
S. O Flaithbheartaigh

Bean an Phiarsaigh
Seán O Mathghamhna
Liam O Maoilíosa
Dr. Brian de Cíosóg
Próinsias O Fathaigh
Aibhistín de Stac
Conchubhar O Coileáin
Eamon de Róiste
P. S. O Cathail
Tomás O Donnchú
Art O Conchubhair
Domhnall O Buachalla
E. Childers
Seoirse Pluingceud
Bean Mhíchíl Ui Cheallacháin
M. P. Colivet
Seán O Ceallaigh
Dr. O Cruadhlaoich
Tomás O Deirg
P. S. O Ruthléis
Enrí O Beoláin
Tomás Maguidhir
Seán Mac an tSaoi
Dr. P. O Fearáin
Seumas O Daimhín
Próinsias Mac Cárthaigh
Seosamh Mac Donnchadha
P. S. O Maoldomhnaigh
P. S. O Broin
Cathal Brugha
Eamon O Deaghaidh
Seumas Mac Roibín
Dr. Seumas O Riain
Seán Etchingham

Seumas O Dubhghaill
Seán T. O Ceallaigh
Pilib O Seánacháin
Bean an Chléirigh
Constans de Markievicz
Cathal O Murchadha
Máire Nic Shuibhne
Domhnall O Ceallacháin
Dr. Eithne Inglis
An t-Oll. W.F.P. Stockley

Appendix V

Letters to Paul Galligan from
Arthur Griffith and Michael Collins

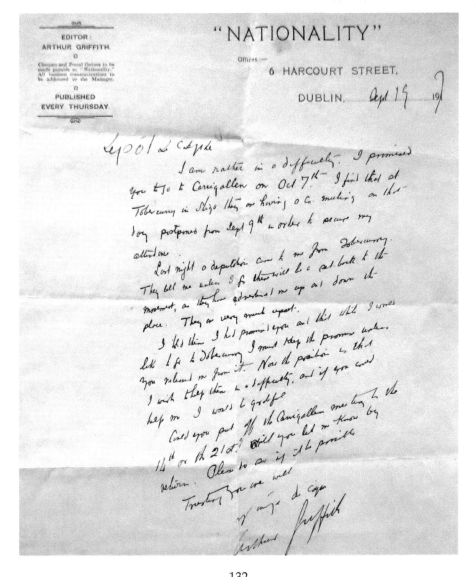

Dáil Éireann.

| Aireact Airgid. | Department of Finance. |

Seoltar Litreaca cun Runaide Dáil Éireann, f/c Tige an Áro-Maoir, Át-Cliat.

Correspondence may be addressed to the Secretary, Dáil Éireann, c/o Mansion House, Dublin.

6, Sraid Fhearchair,
Ath-Cliath,
Lughnasa, a 26, 1919.

P. Galligan, Esq., T.D.,
in Belfast Jail.

A chara,

I enclose you copy of resolution of protest which
was passed at the session of the Dail on Tuesday and Wednesday last. This will be of interest to you. It has
specially been sent to America. I notice in the paper
this morning that you have been put into the criminal
wing in Belfast and I shall be glad to hear how matters
progress with you.

Please report an the situation as often as possible. If there is anything at all we can do, let me
know.

Do chara go buan,

Miceál O Coileáin

AIRE AIRGID.

MC/EL.

Appendix VI

Letters from Peter Galligan

Letter 1 – Letter from Peter Galligan to his son Paul Galligan

6 June 1917

Drumnalaragh
Ballinagh, Co. Cavan

My Dear Paul,

I received your very welcome letter early last week. Once again, I thank God that you are keeping in good health and if rumours are true it takes a man with an iron constitution to withstand and tied over the hardships of prison life especially since you were put on a poor diet and that you are now in solitary confinement. I hope and trust in God all this will soon come to an end and that the Government will see their way to release all prisoners before the convening of the Conference which is to solve the Irish problem? That is if it is ever going to be solved. Dear knows it is time a start was made after centuries of trouble and suffering. But cheer up old man, don't be down-hearted, God will pull you through all your sufferings. And the day of your home coming will bring joy and gladness to all your friends.

I have just returned from Lough Derg and need hardly tell you that I look forward to this yearly pilgrimage to the shrine of St. Patrick as one of the happiest events of my whole life although it is a great penance to fast on bread and water for three days, (on three meals) and perform the holy stations in your bare feet over the sharp stones and rocks which abound on your journey around the stations. And from the thousands who performed this station year after year since the days of St. Patrick, not a murmur is heard. They go through the suffering to make reparation to God for their past sins. And the sins of their departed friends who was near and dear to them or perhaps for some lonely prisoner who is hungry and perhaps starving in his lonely cell. They pray that the God of miracles who multiplies the loaves and fishes will multiply your loaves and sustain you through this awful crisis.

I met a gentleman on the Island from Belfast who is married to a niece of Owen MacNeill, a fine specimen of an Irish man and I may add a true son of St. Patrick. There were many others from Belfast who performed stations and recited prayers for the poor prisoners of Lewes. I assure you that none were forgotten on that Island of prayers and sanctity – I could go on forever praising this holy Island.

Peg's letter was here on my return together with Enniscorthy notes. I also enclose notes from Vera Barry and Mrs. Barry. I am happy to inform you that we are all in good health and spirits here, and we never cease from praying for God to keep you in good health and that your spirits may be ever light. All your friends in Ballinagh are A1 and all pray for your speedy release which they hope will not be long delayed. Peg informed me in her note that Miss O'Flanrahan has not yet got the P.C. I got no word from R. Cycle since February last. You didn't tell me if you had a note from him. I wrote to Mrs. Fagan re. money some time ago and have not heard from her yet, however, I believe she is honest and intends paying but she is no hurry. You need not feel anxious about me giving any of your letters for publication. I would never think of doing such a thing.

With love from all your friends including your affectionate father

P.P. Galligan

Letter 2 – Letter from Peter Galligan to his son Monsignor Eugene Galligan

Drumnalaragh
Ballinagh, Co. Cavan

7 July, 1918

My Dear Eugene,

Just a line to inform you that Paul has been arrested on the fourth incidence at 3.30 in the morning at home - by 8 police and 12 soldiers. Things are a bit lively at present in the old country. Paul committed no crime beyond being an ardent worker for the Sinn Féin cause. Indignation is running very high here at present owing to the handed action of the Irish Government. The country is inundated with castle proclamations and it appears the orange men are to be given a free hand to hold meetings on the 12th. While the croppys have to lie down. We are all well thank God.

With love from your affectionate father,

P. Galligan

🙚 🙚 🙚

Letter 3 – Letter from Peter Galligan to Monsignor Eugene Galligan

Drumnalaragh
Ballinagh, Co. Cavan

9 September 1920

My Dear Eugene,

Just a line to inform you that Paul has been again taken prisoner. A party of 10 armed police arrived here by motor on last Tuesday at 5 p.m. Paul was in the kitchen just after our tea. Paul rushed out the back door pursued by four armed soldiers who fired several shots at him at short range. He got as far as McCann's garden gate and while in the act of opening the gate a rifle bullet went right through his arm. So he was easy prey for the bloodhounds. The bullet went right through the fleshy part of the arm between the elbow and wrist. Such savagery I never witnessed. They wouldn't give me time to have his wound dressed or allow him into the house but dragged him into the motor and drove to Cavan. Dr. Clarke dressed the wound after his arrival. He motored out here yesterday to inform me that Paul was alright and probably Belfast was his destination. I do not have any information as yet of his whereabouts. And he must be prevented from writing or I'd have a letter from him this morning.

I was laid up myself for a fortnight and he nursed me through to good health again. Only to be shot before my eyes. What a mysterious way England shows her love for Irish men by shooting them on site. As soon as I get word from Paul I will write you more fully. Ellen and Jonnie are stricken with grief at the tragedy. But God will pull us through. I am not very strong myself for some time and poor Paul, my sole consolation being now snatched from me is a cruel blow. But God in his mercy will sustain us all. I would give all I possess in this world or every hope to have in it, to be a young man again (God's will be done).

With love from all,

Your affectionate father

P. Galligan.

Appendix VII

Letters from Paul Galligan

Letter 4 – From Paul Galligan to his father Peter Galligan (Written from Dartmoor Prison)

Thursday, 1 June 1916

Governors Note: 'Prisoner will be able to write another letter in four months' time, calculated from date of conviction'.

My Dear Dad,

I know you will be watching for a line from me so I am writing at the very earliest possible date. We arrived here yesterday after a long train journey but the day was fine and we enjoyed it. The prison is built on a big plain but I believe a healthy spot but we felt lonely leaving Mountjoy. I hope you got the letter I sent you, it was just a hurried line. As I heard no news from home since I left I hope everyone is well and in good form.

Now I am feeling in good spirits as we have got settled down at last, as there was nothing more disagreeable as being shifted about and when we get in on the rules and ways here we will be quite at home and won't find the time passing until we are at home again. I had Mrs. Barry to see me at Mountjoy and she told me some of the news and the excitement there was but we had only about 15 to talk, after she waiting for hours to see me. I told her to tell you to pay my insurance for me and I got the receipt book sent to Miss Hyland to send to you. It is 5/- a month and April and May have to be paid for also. Be sure when writing to get him to send you on bonus form for last year. If you have got my trunk you will find the insurance policy enclosed in a large envelope with 'bonus' pinned on and it will explain to you what is missing. The address to send money, to Mr. Rampkin, Pearl Insurance Company, Amiens Street, Dublin. I wrote to him earlier in the year regarding 'bonus' but got no reply and if he does not send it on, write to the chief office in London about it.

Now as regards financial matters, I want you to take over this and to invest it for me as you wish. There is I think a fortnights or perhaps less salary at Bolgers and while I am dealing with Enniscorthy I want to know if you got my trunk and things up yet. I wrote to the girl in my department, Ms. Kavanagh, when in Richmond, to tell the chap in the room, Mr. Kavanagh to pack all my things and to send them to you. I also mentioned the pair of boots and Field Glasses which I left in Lar Lynches of George's Street, Enniscorthy. That is you should have two pairs of boots of mine and see that you get the glasses as they are a valuable pair and he can have no excuse as he took charge of them himself. I want you to see you get these glasses. I also lent Mr. Kavanagh a Grum 3 speed bicycle and I want you to see you get this also, but when you get it you can sell it for me. It is not an old machine and very solid, not unlike your own. There is also as well as the trunk, a suitcase and a hand bag. Fitzsimons Bros. on Ormond Quay Dublin has my own bicycle and you can sell it also if you wish as I am under the impression it would be used there and if you bring it home it will be rode by every lad around so I think you can sell that one too. There is also money owed to me by Quinn and Garadice for a bike but I wrote to the man who runs Fitzsimons, Mr. White about it in the week before I left and up to then I got no reply. So you want to see him about it and he will get it for you. How much it is I do not know as my a/c book with those things in it was taken from me. But he will know and you can rely on him to tell you the truth. But you need not mention the book being lost. I think it is £3 or £3-10-0.

Now, as regards the money that is with Mrs. Fagan. In April, 1915 I lent her £50 at 6% and the terms were £1 per week and interest to be paid every April to Christmas last. At Christmas I was only paid £9-10-0 or £10. At Christmas I got £1 and that makes it either £10-10-0 or £11 as well as things she done which includes two shirts, one pair of puttees, one small flag and a 'Moth' written on linen. Also, when her son was going to Australia I lent her £20 of which I was only paid £5, that leaves £15 to be paid making in all about £55. I'm afraid her place came in for some of the destruction so it may be hard to get money for a while but what I would suggest is to write to her and make some arrangements about being paid a certain sum monthly. And when you have made some arrangements to your satisfaction see that she keeps to it as you will find there will be many excuses for non payment, just as I did, but owing to the friendship between us it was impossible to push for payment. As regards the £50 at 6%, I lent this to her at a time when she was sorely in need of it and knowing from my former experience of not being paid the money I gave when the son was going away, I told her I had borrowed this £50 for her at the 6% on the terms above with the result that I was paid only £10-10-0 or £11, nothing since Christmas, but I have made up my mind that the interest should be paid every April and I think you should write and say that now as I am here you have got to pay the interest from whom I borrowed it and that you are also pressed to keep the former arrangement of paying a pound weekly and that you ask her to meet you in this as best she can as you think it unfair to have to pay the money yourself. Her address is 44 Henry Street or at least it was before the trouble.

There is just one more money matter, when Joe in Drumcrow bought the land, Sarah asked me to give him £30 which I did and he asked me to take some of it some time ago, but as I had a strong regard for Joe and seeing I could put it to no use myself, I told him to keep it for a while and he said he would give it to me this year. So when you are speaking to him tell him I intend starting for myself when I come out and to pay it to you when he can spare it.

Before I pass from the money matters, I told you everything and made it as clear as I could and while I am here I give you over all my money and possessions to invest them. Take charge of them. I give you entire control of everything and to act in any matters concerning me according to your own wishes to open all my letters and to answer any of them you think necessary. When writing to Ms. Kavanagh in Enniscorthy, I asked her to send on any of my letters to Richmond barracks but I did not get a single letter. When you are writing to Bolger you might ask him to send on my letters and if any of them are in reference to business send them back to him again. If they have been sent to Richmond you should write there and get them if possible as there may be some money in them.

There is just another matter which I want to open my heart to you about and that is my engagement to Ms. Hyland. I don't know if you will be surprised at this but when I went down to Enniscorthy I missed her a good deal and when I was in the city that Christmas we settled up things. When I was at home I intended to tell you all but I thought the recent events would make her change her mind but instead she hunted for me for two days at the risk of losing her post. When she found that the word 'convict' was stamped on me for five years, she took it bravely and said she would wait for me and I appreciate her even more now. As you know, as I do, that very few would have done it. She did all in her power to prevent me and was always at me to give up what she knew would lead to trouble and her last words to me was imploring me to follow her advice which I did not do. She may not be the sort of girl you would like me to choose but she is a good religious girl and we are very much attached to each other and after all Dad, money is not everything. I am sure we will be very happy for a girl who makes such a sacrifice for a boy must be truly sincere. Now, I want you to write to her and say you have had a letter from me as she will be anxious to hear about me and ask her if she has anything to say to me so that she may write to you and let you know before you write to me. I can only write and receive one letter every six months so you need not be in a hurry writing and when you do write, send me all the news and write a good long letter as you are not limited like me to a number of pages. So I would expect a long letter. When you are in the city, don't forget but see Peg (Ms. Hyland) and help to cheer her up as you don't know how lonely she is now. So, like everything else I have her in your hands but I hope it won't be the case of doing 'best man' for you when I come out.

Now, about home, how is everyone, remember me to all as I cannot ask for specials as space won't allow. Tell Jonnie not to worry about me as I am enjoying this like a holiday. I am sure my arrest was a great surprise but please God I will soon be home again. Don't forget when you are saying the Rosary to remember me and I here in my lonely cell won't forget you, after all, our religion is all we have left now and it is our only conciliation. I will now say goodbye and may God bless you all.

Best love from your fond son, Paul.

Letter 5 – From Paul Galligan to his brother Monsignor Eugene Galligan
(No address – probably Dartmoor Prison)

September 26, 1916

Prison Dated: October 11, 1916

My Dear Brother,

I cannot tell you how sorry I was to hear from father that you were laid up for some time with a slight attack of flu, but thank God it was not severe and that you were able to say Mass on Easter Sunday. I hope you took a good long holiday to recoup yourself and that you are feeling in your old form again. It was a pity you could not get home for a few months as your native air as well as the sea trip would have worked wonders but that is a pleasure still before you and one we are looking anxiously forward to and when that date comes please God I hope to be in a more hospitable position to receive you than I am at present.

I am sure you were surprised when Father wrote you and said that the brand of the convict was on me for five years but people think I escaped very lightly. I won't trouble you now even if space would allow any of the details of which I know you are already acquainted with, all the circumstances from other sources. How we would laugh a few years ago if someone said 'what a difference in those two brothers, one is destined for the Church and the other for the prison'. Father will be able to keep you posted on all knowledge appertaining to our release, for here we have no knowledge of the doing of the outside world.

You are anxious to know how I am getting along here. I am exactly four months in prison and under the circumstances I feel quite content. Needless to say I feel quite lonely at times for no matter how strong a will power you may possess you will find your thoughts back to times that are past – to the old home and to those that are nearest and dearest. But this is only what you might expect when you consider the many long and dreary hours we have to ourselves. I never felt in better spirits or do I ever remember enjoying better health, thank God for this 'gift of gifts'. Perhaps my indoor life as well as my total abstention from alcohol and tobacco are now tilting in my favour or perhaps the air is responsible for we are about five thousand feet above sea level as well as having the advantage of being situated in a vast woodless moor so you can imagine in your own mind what a pure fresh breeze we get here.

Father was over to see me a fortnight ago. I need not tell you I was delighted to see him. Shut off as I am from the outside world for four months it seems he had dropped down from heaven. I was so glad to see him and talk to him. He

himself will be able to tell you all the news of that brief interview. He is quite delighted with the home and indeed he may
well be proud of it as there is nothing in our parts to equal
it for miles around. He is just after getting the painting complete which I think he said was the finishing touch but there
is just one thing more required to make it complete and that is
a good housekeeper and if she is not there soon to take things
in hand I am afraid many articles will be valueless but this is
a matter I should not have mentioned and as he is there now
himself I expect he is the best judge of this domestic question.

There are a good many things and subjects I would like to
write to you about but I must remain silent and circumstances
compel me to reserve them for another occasion. I go to communion every Sunday and assist at Benediction every Sunday
evening and like every true Irish heart in sorrow and trouble
I turn to the Sacred Heart of Jesus and Mary 'Our 'Mother of
Sorrows' without consolation which not even our own dearest
and nearest can give nor are we disappointed, for in return we
receive that tranquil peace and sympathy which none in this
world can give.

Here in our lonely cells our Rosary beads are our constant
companion and with that emblem of our faith to which our
forefathers held so assiduously to in the past and though the
days were numerous and the hours dark, this simple gift has
brought them victorious through all and why should not we,
dear brother in those dark and lonely hours hold on to that
maternal gift with the same fidelity and love as our forefathers
did in the past. In the evenings as decade after decade slips
through our fingers we raise our hearts to Mary and thank
her for that priceless gift which she gave our forefathers and
which now brings such sweet sympathy and compassion to
our souls. Our chaplain told us yesterday 'Sunday' that our
Holy Father the Pope has asked that the month of October
should be a month of special devotion and prayer to Mary. I
can assure you dear Brother that in no part of the world will
that prayer be more promptly answered or by more fervent

lips or pure souls than the Irish hearts here who are already devoted to Mary.

My convict instinct tells me that the clock will soon strike the hour that says 'stop' and as I am writing against time forgive writing and mistakes and I hope you will be able to make it out. When writing again, write me a short note and write small. Father will enclose it in his next letter. I smile when I think I must send my Christmas greetings in this letter but alas such is the fate of the convict but when you think of the dislocation of the shipping world it may not be so far away from Christmas when you receive it. Before I say goodbye, won't you think of me in your prayers, for remember I never forget you and if it is not too much to ask won't you sometimes remember the convict Paul in your masses.

Goodbye dear brother and may God bless you and send you a very happy and holy Christmas.

With fond love (the clock has just struck)

From your affectionate brother Paul

&❧ &❧ &❧

Letter 6 – From Paul Galligan to his father Peter Galligan

Lewes Prison

20th December 1916

I arrived here last night after a long train journey, I think about 250 miles and was not sorry when we reached the end. Of course as you are already aware all the Irish prisoners will be here together this morning for the first time. I met all my Dublin comrades which were in Portland and as it was the first day we were allowed to talk I need hardly say we had a lot to say to each other and on the whole a great comparing of notes. It seemed so strange to be allowed to talk and walk together and I need hardly say we took full advantage of the privilege and started off a rate that would soon pull up, for the seven long months our tongues were tied for many reasons. I know you are anxious to hear about my health and I must say I never enjoyed better, thank God. I feel just the same as when you visited me at Dartmoor, in fact I have never been unwell since. I hope to have the same good health here as I think we are nearer to the sea than at Dartmoor. Although the prison here is on a pretty high hill, still we were some 1,500 feet higher at Dartmoor. Of course strictly speaking this is not a convict prison but a large country prison. I expect we will get more outdoor exercise here than at Dartmoor. On the whole things here will be more pleasant.

I am writing after a few hours of prison life here and as yet I am not fully acquainted with the rules, but my next letter will be able to give you more news. I expect this is only the first step in the betterment of our condition and in a short time we will expect to be enjoying many privileges, in fact I myself believe this is a great stride towards the end which with things moving so rapidly it may be a good deal is nearer than many of us think. You may say that I am an optimist but I am not.

I received your letter enclosed in Peg's and indeed I expected a much longer one. Get it out of your head because you are enclosing it in Peg's letter that it must therefore only be a note. In future send me all the news you can for you don't know how we look forward to receiving a letter and the longer it is the better we like it. According to our new rules here we are allowed to write and receive a letter once a month and visit once a month also, so that you can write immediately when you get this and you can visit me any time you like after this date. But I don't know if a visiting order is necessary, but if you will let me know when writing about what time I may expect you I will get you sent a visiting order if it is required.

In your last letter you spoke of hopes you had of Jimmy getting tied up before Christmas and I expect this happy event has taken place before now, but as it is not certain I won't say anything that will make him blush. I knew Fr. Pat Reilly when he was in the Parish as I had the pleasure of serving mass for him on several occasions and of course I knew Fr. Tom in Cavan and the last time I saw him was at Maynooth at Fr. Peter O'Reilly's ordination. Indeed, I must say you could not have made a more careful selection and I am sure she will be all that a wife should be and I am sure you are not sorry to have a good housekeeper if she has already taken up her post. I am more than glad to hear that Eugene is alright again and I can quite understand his sympathy for me but tell him not to worry that I never felt in better spirits than at present and how could it be otherwise as the day seems brighter for us as well as the great encouragement we receive from latter events. Certainly since the first day of my prison life I never felt my heart so light. I think I may reverse matters and say you worry a good deal more than I do. I was more than anxious about receiving your last letter as I was worried about your health and I am delighted that you are back to your old self. I don't accept your own word for it but Peg told me in her letter that you returned a different man, that you were greatly improved, in fact she could not believe such a change possible in so short a time.

I'm afraid you gave yourself endless worry over the house and now that it is finished and things settled up satisfactorily you should rest on your oars and let others do the work and you should take a holiday with Fr. Peter from time to time. I am very sorry to hear that Ellen is not feeling well, of course rest is the great thing she wants if you can prevail on her to lie up, but I know too well how hard that will be. As you are on the spot I know that everything will be done to relieve this noble soul who has been more that a Mother to us. Tell her I pray for her both night and day. Tell Jonnie not to worry and that when I get out I have several new inventions for him.

If you think the weather too cold or there is any risk in travelling I will ask you not to come but you will understand those things much better than I do. But if you decide to come, get a slip of paper and put down all the questions you want to ask me so that you won't leave without getting all the news you want. Remember me to all it is impossible to give you all the names and when writing be sure to send me all news as well as all the messages you get for me. I hope you are taking good care of Peg for me. I am rushing this letter to get it away with the first available post with the hope that it may be in time for Christmas day, for I know how anxious you are to get a letter. I will now say goodbye Dad and may God bless you all and send you a happy and peaceful Christmas and though I am not with you in person I am in spirit . Again a happy Christmas and a bright new year.

With love, your fond son, Paul.

P.S. When writing to Peg give her any news you think necessary. Write a good long letter and give me all news. Remember me to all who ask for me.

&. &. &.

Letter 7 – From Paul Galligan to his father Peter Galligan

Lewis Prison, March 6 1917

Dear Dad,

After long and weary waiting I get your long letter on February 27 with enclosures from Eugene and Mrs. Barry. I see your letter was written on February 13th but was of course held up in the censor's office, but like all government offices 'red tape' predominates. Well Dad, I must say your long letter atones for the past - you have wiped out by pen and ink a long standing grievance. I am glad you are able to lay hands on foolscap. At least now that you have found it I hope it will last until I go out.

What do you think of Eugene's letter. It has been read by every man here from McNeil down. It has done an amount of good. It consoled the old and fired the young. Although we heard that conscription was defeated in Australia in November, we did not know we had so many friends. We know the Bishop of Melbourne has sent 1,000 dollars but what we appreciate most is the messages of fidelity, love and hope that 'Royal Australia' has sent us. I am proud of Eugene's letter and as it is the first to reach us from Australia it got a welcome no other letter yet got. Several copies have already been asked for, so as to be kept as souvenirs of Royal Australia's vindication. This should be a headline for you in future when writing.

I got Irish books a few days ago and I got none of the Catholic magazines yet. I was sorry to hear that your last trip over to Dartmoor had so bad an effect on your health. In fact I thought it should have a different result and that the sea trip would do you good. In fact I am glad to see you are not thinking of coming over for some time as the time is now cut down to 30 minutes and it is not worth it. I hope your health is not failing for you spoke in your last letter as if you were not yet strong and if so you should again go and see a Dublin specialist because as you know better than anyone that there is nothing to be gained from delay. When writing again tell me all about yourself as I am anxious to know how you are getting on.

Yes, it was a magnificent victory for Plunkett, 3,200 - it is significant. I hope you are not one of the thousand who our friend from Swinford spoke of so lately. He seems to be getting hard knocks these times. We heard at our last war lecture that half a million women were wanted for the front. Drumnalaragh and Knockanore should make a good response. I would like to see Ellen baking in a dug-out, Mary Coby cooking rashers under shell-fire, Biddy Boylan selling cigarettes to the music of machine guns or Margaret Conlan bringing us supplies of tea to the firing line. This scheme is alright from a patriotic view but from a moral point of view what do we see

– girls from the age of 16-25 taken away from all home restrictions, supervision or influence and transferred to camps and kitchens, where under the most strict vigilance they will come in contact with millions of soldiers. Even in Catholic Ireland where Christian ideals has so long fought against this rottenness, we find since the war has started that this putrid war has at last broken down the barriers and touched our sainted land. All I say is that God and Mary guard and protect any Irish Catholic girl whose patriotism may inspire to join.

The governor has just told us that tomorrow is going to be devoted to the discussion of the Home Rule Bill and I hope even at the eleventh hour that Ireland will receive her long deferred nationality but to my mind it will only be a discussion. I am glad to hear the Freeman has been re-modelled and I hope the latter addition to its staff will fulfil our expectations and I am also delighted to hear that Will Martins' dreadful has thrown off the garb of neutrality.

Thank God the cold and misery of winter is passing and we are glad to see a little sunshine again. But the awful price of food stuff and the coldness of winter, the poor must have suffered awful and still the prices keep going up. Here they will soon know what 46-48 was like.

I am glad you and Ms. King has become so good friends. I told her brother here what you said. We had a few jokes at your expense as well as coming to the decision that pilgrimages is not got up for prayers. I am glad to hear that the machinery for Kill coal mine is on its way, you should have things humming soon. Of course three thousand pounds is not much capital for a coal mine but is a good start. The co-op system is a good idea and on the whole it should work out well. I expect you will be able to book orders soon. Give me all particulars in your next as I am very much interested in it as it is so near home. Of course I have been spouting to the boys here of what Cavan is doing for industry. I see you have not bought any cattle yet, perhaps it is all for the best. I heard that there was a fall in cattle during February which was owing to the very high insurance as well as the high and uncertainty of transit and this to a large extent would be responsible for the absence of so many English buyers but this fall is only temporary and you may expect a big rise again soon if you have not had it already. I was sorry to hear you had trouble with the walls but the plan you adapted was the best and of course you might as well do it at once and be finished.

There is no sign of the war being finished yet, in fact we are being told that it may soon be carried on in a longer scale as America is expected to soon come in on the side of the allies but only waiting for the 'Overt Act'. Three weeks ago we thought it had arrived when a black was drowned. Next day one of our humorist said Congress asked Wilson what he was going to do and his reply was 'it was to be kept dark'. Next week we were told a missionary was drowned and again our friend came up smiling and told us that Wilson's reply to Congress was 'there was too much preaching'. Last week we were told that a Cunard liner was sunk and that a sailor was lost. Now we thought our friend the humorist was 'floored' but to our surprise he came up with a bigger smile than ever and told us that Wilson told Congress 'he was not a sailor that could not swim'. We are still waiting for 'Overt Act', so much talked about.

You will be surprised to get this letter so soon compared with delay of our latter letters. The censorship is now done here by the governor not in London at the censor's office which indeed is a great advantage to us and for which we must thank the governor. We are getting along splendid with the Irish, in fact since I last wrote to you I have not opened any other but Irish books. Don't be afraid I won't waist the opportunity.

About money matters I am surprised at the attitude of Joe Reilly. Let Jimmy see him again and if no good results I will write to him. As regards Miss Fagan, I know from my own experience that I writing would do no good, the only result would be a plausible letter. If you keep writing to her it is the only chance of getting something. Yes Dad, I answer with you, God save me from my friends. I have learned many things during the last twelve months. Experiences sometimes bought dear but now the brass is separated from the gold. I am writing a note to Mrs. White. I am glad you kept the bike as it is dear to me on account of my once famous ride. I am glad all at home is so good and that Mick Reynolds is alright. Again, remember me to them all. Tell Johnny I am glad to hear he has thrown away the stick, I suppose the next thing I will hear of himself and Margaret getting tied. Give my love to Johnny, Paddy and Ellen, also to all the boys and girls.

With fond love from your son Paul

My dear brother,

This is a much shorter than I had intended but I never felt myself creeping down the page. Certainly you sent me a good page of news and I hope father will receive that page from you in future. Remember as many as like can write on foolscap. I got Irish books alright, on going through them I say some old names which brought back some happy days. I am glad such a change has taken place in St. Patrick's, long may it continue.

With reference to Ballinagh Boys that went up to Belfast for Government examination that they passed with flying colours and are now in Armagh on three months approbation. Give not only mine and Sullivan's congratulations to the relations but I am asked to do so on behalf of every man here. Give my regards as well as Sullivan's to Charlie and Nora. I am glad to hear you are thinking of settling down, well I hope I may yet be home for that day. I am glad you have an eye on the sharks but they are now super sharks. Now I will expect as long a letter from you as last and with as much news told, if not more for you come to know better than father what style of news interests me. Now, goodbye and best wishes from Sullivan and self to all the boys.

With love from your brother Paul

P.S.

I am sure you are anxious to get the camp photos. If you write to P. McGlynn, 10 Mardyke Street, Athlone, he will, I'm sure, be able to provide them. Tell Jimmy to be sure of 'Nationality' for the next few weeks. Tell me how you like the photo Peg sent you. We had photos here of Kent, McDermott, Connolly, Daly, Colbert, Hewson and expect shortly to have list complete. Writing long letters soon,

Paul

P.P.S.

Special hold over your letter until you get one from Peg to enclose. Love to all from Paul

ॐ ॐ ॐ

Letter 8 – From Paul Galligan to his brother Monsignor Eugene Galligan

Lewes Prison

April 6 1917

My Dear Brother

I was delighted to get your very welcome letter for it was more than I could hope, to get a letter from you so soon for I only received your first letter on February 28 as there is a great delay in censoring, not only our outward letters but also the letters coming to us. I am most grateful to Sr. Julian for her kindness as well as for her thoughtfulness in sending Agnus Deis and card. The card is exquisite and for a convict, most appropriate. God bless her, for them as well as for her prayers and those of her little ones and I will tell you honestly dear brother we require the strength of all your prayers to bring us through the misery and hardship of prison life. It is not easy to sit down and write cheery letters 'the pen writes but the heart dictates, not' but to write otherwise is against rules, but the day will come please God and soon when I will be able to place before you the manipulations of the British convict system. Yes we have seen the drudgery and humiliation of prison life and not only have we tasted the gall of the convict but were made drain the cup to the dregs. Often as I paced my cell at night I asked myself, is there a just God in heaven and turning my eyes to the cross attached to my beads (the only token of religion allowed in Dartmoor) I seem to hear 'forgive them father, they know not what they do' and those words of Christ dying on the cross is the answer and it brings to us Irish convicts the great lesson of perseverance and submission and thus by this humiliation and self sacrifice won his glorious triumph over his enemies.

I know too well that during this long interval I was not forgotten by you and that I always have a share in your prayers and masses and if a poor convicts prayers are heard remember that in a cell in this prison night and morning are prayers offered to Mary to ask her divine son to give you help and strength to carry on his holy mission. I am glad you got photos but I expect father will in a short time be able to send you better ones. I am also asking father to see if he can get the books you speak about. I have his letter finished but I hope if he runs his eye through this that he will send you Dr. O'Dwyer's Lenten Pastoral which I read here and as it is published in pamphlet form it should not be too hard to get. I am sure it would interest you.

I am glad to hear that in far distant shore we have some friends. God bless them and all whose hearts still throb with that on unquenchable love of fatherland. We had a general communion here on St. Patrick's Day. It was glorious to see one hundred and twenty all in prison uniform and on which was stamped the arrow, the official mark of the convict. On both breast was a sprig of shamrock. Some wore a Patrick's harp worked in green, white and orange by some loving sister or fond mother and as they filed past with that military step and manly bearing which twelve months of prison life has not affected and on every face was depicted that devotional look which Irish are known the world over. At the altar they received the blessed sacrament with that reverence and sanctity. Many a heart was sad and many an eye was moist as they thought of their last St. Patrick's Day communion in Ireland and with the dear ones at home and with Jesus in our hearts we ask his father in heaven to look down with pity on our country to protect and guard her and those who are so dear to us and to give us strength to carry his cross patiently to the end. Tears came to my eyes as the priest appeared on the altar with a bunch of shamrocks on his vestments which he wore in honour of our saint as well as to honour his flock who are all Irish. In the evening we had a lovely sermon on the life of St. Patrick and on its conclusion were asked to pray that God and his great mercy would again restore France to the arms of the Catholic church. Before benediction we sung 'Hail Glorious St. Patrick' and never have I heard it sung with such enthusiasm before and the last line 'for God and St. Patrick and our own Native Lord' re-echoed again and again before it finally died away.

The weather here continues almost as severe as at Christmas for that same cold biting northern wind still remains and we have almost continual showers of snow, sleet and rain, in fact snow in parts is almost three foot. Had you any procession on St. Patrick's Day? I expect Fr. Ryan held his annual parade and it was always with pride that I read in the 'Advocate' his enthusiasm and patriotism on these occasions and I regret to say his countrymen lack both, just at present.

It was very kind of Mrs. Ridings to remember me still, convict as I am and I would be grateful if you would convey to her the pleasure I feel at knowing that she remembers me with kindness. As regards work, I have not to labour in quarries but I might tell you that I would prefer it to the work we are on. Never fear we are keeping fit as far as circumstances will allow but being locked up in a cell 16 hours out of 24 don't keep you up to fighting order but thank God the health is splendid and under prevailing circumstances my spirits are a long way above zero. Here we see and realise the great power of prayer and many here have gone through several trying critical operations in the past and were forbidden certain work and food. They have overcome all obstacles and in the face of all hardships have retained that health and spirit that surprise even ourselves and we attribute this to all your prayers. God will reward you for it.

This is Good Friday, we are just after finishing the stations of the cross. This day makes me realise that we are now twelve months in prison for next week is Easter week - so many memories to us all. I suppose out there we are branded cut throats – renegades – anti-Catholic, anti-clerical and the usual category of scurrilous names by which we are known in the Irish press. But names do not harm 'we still smile on'.

How is the population in Australia during this momentous time or are you suffering from the blockade or do you feel the scarcity of food? An undisclosed state like yours should be pouring with food. I don' know if I told you in my last letter that we are allowed Catholic magazines and devotional books so you can send some if you wish. By the kindness of the Governor I am allowed this extra note paper and I must say in justice, that he is a thorough gentlemen and has done everything that duty will allow to make prison life possible to bear. I will ask you not to forget photo when writing, send it as soon as possible. I will again ask you to remember me in your prayers and masses and to ask God to give me strength to carry patiently to the end the bitter and heavy cross of the convict. Good bye dear brother and may God bless you.

Love from your fond brother Paul

Convict 921B

P.S. When writing you are not bound to any certain quantity of paper. Write me a good long newsy letter.

Letter 9 – From Paul Galligan to his brother Monsignor Eugene Galligan

Lewis Prison, England

4 May 1917

My Dear Brother,

Another month has passed since I last wrote you and it only appears as yesterday. In a few days I will be celebrating my first anniversary of my imprisonment and looking back on it, seems so short yet there were times when every minute felt an hour and every hour a year. I always read with horror the sad incidents of suicide but I will never read of a suicide in future without pity and compassion for I know the battles those souls had to fight and it is only our Irish Catholic faith coupled with the prayers and devotion which we learned at our mothers knee that brought us unsullied through it all.

Well dear brother, I don't know what to write for I need hardly tell you that prison is the worst place in the world for news and a wall 30 ft high inspire (with) thoughts for little writing. Of course I could fill books with prison life but we are forbidden to do so and the penalties for the infringement of this rule is pretty severe but this will leave me all the more to tell you when we meet. We get a war lecture every Wednesday and in this we are kept in touch with all the doings in Europe and it is interesting to hear some of the debates as well as the forecasts which I must say comes often pretty near the mark and as some of us are provided with atlases, we can follow the war pretty closely, but just at present, although there is severe fighting going on, things seem to be at a stand-still and as casualty lists are not published it is impossible to guess the losses.

I get a long letter from father every fortnight and in this I get all local and home news. Tomorrow, 5th May is your election day and I expect there is a bit of excitement with your news as you are on the eve of the pole but I hope you will follow up the fine victory you had in November last and we will look forward to next Wednesday to hear the results and on that date, there will be an election in Ireland which I hope you all will be proud of. Last week for the first time, we were allowed Irish Catholic magazines. I need hardly tell you how delighted we were to get some good wholesome reading after the filthy stuff we were getting for 12 months. I never thought that British journalism had fallen so low until I got some of the magazines here. Even the best of them from a literary point of view are far below our Irish magazines, and morally - well the least said about this the better, but one and all attack the Catholic church, some openly and some hide under the flowery language of friendly criticism. I have never got a magazine since I came to prison that had not an article vilifying Ireland, her priests, or her Church, while nearly every second article advocated some 'ism' whose doctrines suited the people of this country and with such a propaganda that in civilised England we find at the taking of the census a short time ago that there was one million who professed no religious belief. It was disgusting to see in those magazines full page photographs of actresses, some almost naked and in such positions as to bring the outline of the figure fully before your gaze and one magazine labelled such filth as this with the title 'Artistic Posses of a Well Known Actress'. Those magazines are supposed to be the 'cream' of British literature and nearly all boast of being read in every house in England. This being so, I am not surprised at the sensation that has been caused by the revelations concerning the male and female population of England and which was proved by statistics last month. Rome, France, who next? 'Wait and see'.

You need not be a bit uneasy as regards my health, I am enjoying far better health than I expected. Under the circumstances I feel quite happy and contented and day by day my heart grows light for where is the Irish heart that does not beat faster and faster as the days go on, for are we not getting nearer and nearer to that goal which we have so long dreamt of. The hour I enjoy most is the time when it grows too dark for reading and too bright for bed. I get my stool up to the window as my cell faces the west, I gaze to where the sun has set on the distant horizon and I follow it until I see it setting behind the Leitrim mountains, just as I used to watch it set at home and if you could get a glance at every cell window at that hour you would see at each, a face without a smile and a body without a soul for during that hour we are back again in Ireland, some sitting again around the fire with a dear wife and loving children, some again are winding their way through the hills and valleys and some hear again the tramp, tramp of marching men which was so sweet to us all. This is an hour that is dear and sacred to us all and often I stay there till a cold night breeze brings me back to realities again. During a dream like this, many are the visions that pass before your view and many are the thoughts, past and present and future that pass rapidly through your mind and many are the questions put aside unanswered only to appear again in a new form but always out of this chaos of thoughts one vision nightly passes before my eyes - it is the figure of Eireann (not as we see it in postcards with a harp in her hand and a crown on her head), her face marked with sorrow on which was still the trace of recent tears but in her eyes with that new look of hope which you only see on a face of one, who battling for life, see hope after hope fade away and who at the eleventh hour see in the distant horizon, aid and succour. On her lips were a smile that brought a thrill to my heart for it was the smile of victory. As she passed I seemed to hear her say 'after prison, freedom'. Such is a dreamer's dream.

I expect father told you about two of our comrades being released, their lives being in danger caused through ill health. One, released now a fortnight, is not able to go to Ireland but is still in a hospital in England, the other is now in a nursing home in Dublin. Owing to the great scarcity of food we are on 'war rations' since 15 April. So you see, the poor convicts have to tighten their belts but God knows they were tight enough before. No matter, take it all smiling, it is in a good cause and you should thank your stars that you people in Australia don't know what war rations is.

We are all studying Irish and we are all making steady progress and hope to have a good knowledge at least when we go out. Don't you think it very kind of Government to give us an opportunity to learn our own language? We had an anniversary mass for our dead comrade last Sunday, 29 April. We had a general communion on the same morning and many and fervent were the prayers that were offered up for those noble souls the purest and the best of Irish manhood and although we feel lonely and sad for such comrades yet we cannot regret them, they have lead a noble life and died a glorious death. The chaplain on giving his sermon paid a warm tribute to them both for their pure lives and splendid death and no matter in what part of the world where there were Irish, no matter what their political opinions were, they would that day join in the universal prayers that were said for them.

I don't know if I mentioned to you that we have a hymn every Sunday evening in Irish. You see though in exile we not only cling to the old tongue but to the music. Don't forget for I mentioned in my last letter about photo and cross and of course any religious books you wish to send, I will get them. Kindly remember me to Mrs. Ridings and also to that noble soul, Sr. Julian. Tell her if she would like to receive it, I will send her a sprig of shamrock that I wore in my cap on Patrick's day. Give my love to all our Australian friends that we don't know. Now goodbye and always remember in your prayers your loving brother,

Convict G216.

P.S. Excuse all the errors and mistakes. I left it for last and at the end had to rush it through. I hope you will be able to make out my writing.

Paul

Letter 10 – Letter from Paul Galligan to his brother Monsignor Eugene Galligan

Drumnalaragh
Ballinagh

October 14, 1917

My Dear Brother,

Don't you think it is about time I should write you. I'm sure you often ask yourself why you did not get a letter oftener - the British Government is the answer. For since I left prison all of my letters outwards and for me, are held up for days: such is the honour afforded me as a convict. I only found out the other day that all the letters that father got for you from prison were two, well I wrote to you first if not most but the news then regarding prison life would not be allowed outside of a prison wall and even at this distant date you would not get this letter if I attempted to relate some of my prison experience. Not but the death of 'Ashe' has laid before the nations of the world what England is, and how sincere her sympathy is for 'small nations'. But when she is done with Ireland she will be sorry she went into the war on behalf of small nationalities. Yes, we got hell in Dartmoor, their very means as well as the influence and power of a full Masonry Prison Board was used to break us up. I have often heard this war spoken as 'hell with the lid off', but the originator of this expression never put a week in with us in Dartmoor jail or he would have added 'and all the past and present generations of English men trying to devour 65 Irish convicts and could not'.

Lincoln was not so bad until we struck work and then we realised that all jails are alike. After Lincoln, I had the pleasure of being moved, in chains, to Parkhurst prison where all the British imbecile convicts together with all the diseased convicts in England. So bad was this prison that we refused to use the lavatories, so prevalent was venereal disease. This will give you an idea of what we had to undergo.

In Parkhust we were placed side by side with the lowest of criminals, thieves and pick-pockets. During my stay in Parkhurst, I had beside me the murderer of the 'Gordon Tunnell Tragedy' who was doing I think ten years and who will be free next year. So you see we had a bit of experience. As I said before, if I quoted all I went through you would not get this letter but some time I will relate you all when we get together.

God bless for your first letter to me in prison. It came to me in an hour when we were low in spirits and when hope was darkest and it was the first ray of sunshine to penetrate our prison wall from outside Ireland. For the first time we heard the good news from Australia that it stood by us and as your letter passed from hand to hand you could see the eye brighten and the head raising for each of them knew that Ireland had a good and true friend in Australia. I was anxious to get your letter for a personal motive as well as national for I did not exactly know what your feeling as regards the war or if like so many more at that date you were against the rising in Easter week. So you can just picture to yourself how one living in such surroundings as Dartmoor, a mind filled with such uncertainty, what a God-send your letter was and don't be a bit vain when I say it was quoted on several platforms in Ireland.

Your last letter I got about nine days ago, the first since I came home. It was written a few days after our release, so you can see it takes a letter three months to go now. It was a good manly letter and only represents a true Irish heart. I have shown it to a good many of my friends who were delighted with it and you will have a warm reception on your return home. I am afraid if I took out your letter I would fill a copy on the data you have given me.

God bless the men who died in Easter week, our casualties, was only 60 plus 16 executed, a total of 76, but if you saw Ireland today you would say it was worth it all for it has gone Sinn Féin mad. Nothing but the full independence of Ireland will satisfy the Irish people. Redmond is a man of the past and his policy is only supported by a dwindling minority and I mean and know what I am saying when I tell you that with the exception of about two seats, we will win all the parliamentary seats at the next election and we are preparing hard and fast for it for I am of the opinion that peace is near at hand and with peace of course comes a general election.

Sinn Féin clubs, at least two and in some cases three already established in every parish, this in itself will give you an idea of what Sinn Féin has accomplished. In nearly all those clubs, Irish classes are standard and Irish dancing is taught, no English song is now ever heard and the greatest Sinn Féiner is the boys and girls from three upwards. Ireland is born over again – baptised in a blood of the martyrs of Easter week. We are at last marching to freedom, glorious freedom, this time the might of England cannot stop our march for neither money nor jobs can buy us. All we want is Ireland free to act and work out her own salvation, in other words an Irish Republic and for that we are willing to die, if again necessary.

Goodbye dear brother with all the love of my faithful heart,

Paul

> > >

Letter 11 – From Paul Galligan to his brother Monsignor Eugene Galligan

November 15, 1917

Drumnalaragh
Ballinagh

My Dear Brother,

Although I made a promise in my last letter that I write to you weekly but, it is now a good month since I wrote before and many things have happened since then and one thing in particular, the Sinn Féin Convention deserves a word. I sent you cuttings from the papers reporting its stages and some photo cuttings as well, I don't know if you got them or not. Of course I was there and it made you feel proud to be a Sinn Féiner to see all the fine young fellows that were there and it would give you food for thought if you stood in the balcony and looked down on the noble, intellectual faces that were below. I would safely say that such noble countenances seldom adorn any parliament but the one thought that struck me most was, 'if the governing of this country was in those men's hands what would we be in five years'.

You have already seen the Convention criticised in the press but one thing we have settled forever, that is that Sinn Féin is not a secret society. We are the first political body in Ireland and perhaps I may add England that allow the press into its meetings and to be present at all its deliberations for this we have gained some support from the press. You have heard all about the 'Ashe' case. The poor fellow, I knew him well. We were in Dartmoor and Lewis together and he was a fine type of a man in every sense of the word but his death was a second 'Easter Week' in this country as regards the change of public opinion. Going away from the Convention (SF) it was attended by 1,700 delegates from 1,000 clubs representing 250,000 members and the unanimous decision of this 1,700 delegates was to demand at the peace conference an Irish Republic and to demand nothing less as we want now to completely sever our connection with England.

Don't believe what you hear as regards a second rebellion in this country. It is all newspaper talk. We know, as the world knows that England cannot afford to have another rebellion and the English press is now trying to do a bit of bluff but for once in her life it is going to fail. We know England's strength, we know our own, but this newspaper talk is not going to keep us from going on with Ireland's work. Organise, Organise, Organise is the word throughout the land today, for we know we have a slippy customer in England and today every parish in

Ireland has got its volunteer corps. as well as its two SF clubs to which is attached an Irish class, an Irish dancing class, Irish history class and a dramatic club.

All the huge correspondence regarding the volunteers clubs, classes, etc. never passes through the post. The SF post office is not newspaper talk, it is a reality and as England pays a censor and staff something like 10,000 a year to look and photograph our letters it must be wearing long faces for the 'sack' now stares them in the face.

I was awfully sorry that Fr. Ryan got away without calling, for I would have just loved to have a good long chat with him as well as I had a number of books, souvenirs to send you back with him but enclosed you will find a letter from Fr. Ryan of Tipp explaining all. I suppose you heard about Stephen Clarke being killed at the front, poor fellow it was not his love for England that brought him out for he was a staunch SF, may the Lord rest his soul. I was speaking to Fr. Matt Dolan who is at present teaching in St. Patrick, Cavan at the Convention. He is a grand little man and he is going on the Chinese mission. I says to Fr. Matt, 'Ireland cannot afford to lose such as you' but he says 'it won't be long until I am back again to an Irish Republic'. 'God bless you but God bless you as a lay man can work for the salvation of your country'.

Now for home news. Dad is getting along fine and he is improving daily and few and far between is his heart attacks. In fact he is out digging potatoes daily now, so that is no bad sign. Jimmy is just his usual, is causing father a good deal of worry which I don't want to get into. Dad thinks if he got married he would be alright. But that will all depend on his wife as he himself is very obstinate. Jonnie, Ellen and Paddy are all grand, yet Ellen got very stooped but otherwise in good health. I did not start work myself yet and just as I was thinking of it, I got elected to the governing body of Sinn Féin for South Leitrim so you see if I go on this Body, as I am in honour bound to as now, I would have to give up work so at present I am just idling my time away. I will now say goodbye and Dad, Jimmy, Jonnie join in wishing you a very happy Christmas.

With fond love from you affectionate brother,

Paul

꙳   ꙳   ꙳

Letter 12 – Letter from Paul Galligan to his brother Monsignor Eugene Galligan

Drumnalaragh
Ballinagh

29 November 1917

Dear Brother,

I am just after getting your letter of the 6 September and I cannot tell you how glad I was to get it. Now before I start, I think I told you in my first letter that the Government pay special attention to all my letters so you see it keeps me from saying all I would like to say and if I wrote to you a full account of the rebellion, it would perhaps be used against me or others as evidence at a later stage, but as you are so anxious for details I will give you a few facts regarding Easter week. Of the volunteer movement which was responsible for the rising, you know all about it. During the war we drilled and armed openly and this, after Redmond had tried to break the movement. 17 March 1916 was fixed as a parade day for the Dublin battalions. The efficiency, the equipment, enthusiasm and determination of the volunteers opened the eyes of the Government and from that hour the Government determined to suppress the I.V. but how was the question, as we were armed and disciplined. As time went on the Government and their spies, the 'G' men were making things hot and we knew the hour was coming when we would have either to surrender our arms or fight for them. If we gave them up we knew too well we were surrendering the last shred of Irish nationality and we knew we had to fight to keep Ireland from becoming an English province. We knew it was Ireland's last chance but we were to wait till an hour when the Government was in a fierce struggle with Germany and when she would either have to withdraw troops to Ireland or give us all we demanded. Preparations were made with all haste.

The Volunteers training was gone into in detail and each company was classified. Snipers, engineers, red cross, armoury, etc. and in a few months such efficiency was attained that as yet the British army has not attained. It cannot be denied that we were in close communication with Germany. Good Friday was not the day as many believed but Saturday before the arrival of the arms ship and why it failed was that she arrived 36 hours before her time. If she had arrived as arranged all would have been well.

On Easter Sunday the Volunteer was to act as arranged but on Good Friday the arms ship was sunk and many of us saw that its sinking was fatal to the rising, timed for Easter Sunday. But from this on, things travelled fast. After the news of the sinking of the vessel it was decided to postpone the event but now the Government made the pace. The Privy Council met in the Lord Lieut. house in the park and it was there they decided to get 300 of the officers of the Volunteers arrested. A meeting of the Military Council of the Volunteers was called and it was decided to fight for this reason, that Monday would see all the Volunteer officers arrested and a general lifting of arms would take place. For once the officers were gone, the Volunteers would only be a mob, and it was easier to go and take a position than fight for it.

From Easter Sunday it was a race between us and the Government but we got there first even if it was only with a small force. I came up to Dublin from Enniscorthy on Saturday (Easter Saturday) and remained in town until 3 a.m. on Tuesday, when I left for Wexford with final orders. Being in Dublin during the crisis I was at meetings, some of the facts of which I cannot write here as this letter I am sure will be censored, but all the leaders I knew intimately and I saw P.H. Pearse, W. Pearse, Connolly, Plunkett, and McDermott at the GPO for the last time on Tuesday morning. I left Dublin by bike as no motor could be got or spared but was told a motor would be at Naas. But when I arrived there I found that no County was in arms but Dublin.

After cycling day and night, I arrived at Enniscorthy on Wednesday. Here men were ready to fight but the Officer commanding Wicklow, Wexford, Carlow, Kilkenny, Waterford refused to accept Pearse's orders as MacNeill was Chief of Staff (here let me say that MacNeill did what he thought was right and what I myself would have done was I in his position) and would take no orders from Pearse. This was the position when I got to Enniscorthy. I immediately called a Conference of the Officers and placed the situation before them together with the orders I got. I told them as I then knew that only Dublin was fighting and also said that it was only a matter of time, but all the officers of Wexford decided to fight if it was only for 12 hours, as they would not stand by and see their brothers in Dublin fall without striking a blow.

At this Conference our Secret Service Department sent in a report that two troop trains were ready at Wexford awaiting the landing of a troop ship from England. This was the turning point, for the Wexford Officers said it would be to the everlasting disgrace of Wexford if they stood by and allowed a train with troops to pass through. All was unanimous in fighting. Mobilising orders were at once dispatched and after a few hours more spent in the study of maps, etc. we fired the first shot at 5 a.m. on Thursday morning and the Republican flag was hoisted at 12 exactly amidst great cheering. I, as Senior Officer as well as by authority from Pearse took command and was responsible for all things in Enniscorthy till the order for surrender arrived on Sunday morning at 7 a.m.

At that time the English troops were at Wexford town, only 15 miles away. At first we would not take the word of the Officer who brought Pearse's surrender order and we immediately sent two Officers to interview Pearse in Dublin. At

12 on Monday, the Officers all surrendered. I may say we only mobilised 200 on Thursday and at 12 noon on Sunday we had over 1,000 men and if Pearse had held out for a month and that the South had risen, I say it now nearly two years after the fight, it was hard to know how things would have gone, for at that time England had no artillery in Ireland and for once we met them man to man and as man to man we could beat them 5 to one.

As you may now see by reading this that the line from Wexford to Dublin was the principal line of which England would move troops and for that reason as well as others that we held it. One word before I finish the Rebellion, and if it is to say that what you heard and read about Casement is English slander and I say that when the history of the Rebellion comes to be written, no man shall shine brighter than that of Roger Casement next to P.H. Pearse. I love him for I know the terrible sacrifice to prove his love to Ireland. It was from Pentonville Prison where he was hanged, we were released and I had the honour to kneel over his grave and there I prayed for God to give me strength to follow his principles to the end. Perhaps this you may not know, that when R. Casement asked to be received into the Catholic Church his request was refused by Cardinal Burke unless he made a statement repudiating all his actions. R. Casement refused this action of C. Burke to interfere with his politics. The matter was brought before the Pope to where also C. Burke was summoned and he was told that his first duty as Cardinal was to his God and never in future to allow himself again to be made a cat's paw of the British Government.

I was Court Marshalled on May 14th and sentenced to be shot. This was at Richmond Barracks. I was then brought down to Kilmainham Jail and I was locked up in a cell there to await either the execution of my sentence or to have it commuted. In Kilmainham we got only a blanket and had to sleep on the floor and got only dry biscuits and soup to eat. On Sunday I think it was, the 21 May an Officer came to my cell and said the OC, the forces in Ireland commuted my sentence to five years. In fact I was sorry, for I was prepared for the death and it would have been a relief then as the whole week of the Rebellion I had not a single hours sleep and when then on 21 May after sleeping for three weeks on cold floors and in your clothes without a change, death was preferable to another week of it. I, with others was changed to Mountjoy prison on 22nd and I thought it was heaven to get a bath and a clean shirt. Here things were not too bad, the wardens were hounds but had a soft heart.

On 29 May, MacNeill and I and about 10 others were brought to England in a cable boat. On May 30 at 4 p.m. we were safely lodged in Dartmoor Jail. Here there was 57 and 55 more were in Portland. No description of Dartmoor would give you an idea of what it is, the nearest approach is an expression now often read in reference to the war 'Hell with the lid off'. I wish to say no more about it as it was the worst we had to contend with and enough to drive me mad. It left its stamp on us that time will never efface.

On December 20th I was brought to Lewis where things were made a bit easier for us, but we came to the conclusion that if we went on nice and quietly we would be there forever so we kicked up a row that made us famous all over the world. On June 12th 1917 I was removed to Parkhurst in the Isle of Wight as I was a bad hospital case and on June 17 came the glorious news of our release. Back to Ireland to continue to the work we left unfinished, back to Ireland to give another hand in the rising of the Republican flag and when it goes up again it will never come down and I may say as a final word, when that day comes there will be no prison, no jail 'Freedom or Death'. This is just a few incidents in our fight and some day, please God, around the fire in the far distant land of Australia, I will give you more details which I cannot write. I will tell you about deeds which have yet to be equalled but must remain in oblivion, because we are only poor uneducated and ill-advanced young men.

Letter 13 – From Paul Galligan to his brother Monsignor Eugene Galligan

Drumnalaragh
Ballinagh
'Good Friday' March 29th, 1918

My Dear Brother,

Perhaps if I was in jail you would hear from me more often, but with going here and going there it is hard to get writing. I know you are thirsting for news regarding this dear land of ours but with such a censorship, it would be impossible to speak out one's mind, for if I did – well it is just a chance if you would get it. My last letter was a long one and covered a good deal of ground regarding Easter, etc. but did you get it? Things are going well in Ireland and Dr. Mannix's last speech was of great help to us here. We quoted it from platform, at dance and crossroads. Until now, Dr. Mannix and Irish Freedom go side by side here.

Dr. Hallin has taken Dr. O'Dwyer's place as Bishop of Limerick and has come out and taken his stand by Sinn Féin, so we are gaining ground every day and you need not mind the defeat that we got in Armagh and Waterford, this means nothing and both will be won in a general election. I am going in the morning to Tyrone to give a helping hand but it also is a helpless job as we are out numbered five to one, that is the combined vote of unionists and party, for there is no unionists now as they are all one where Sinn Féin is concerned, but we expect to win Kings County by a handsome majority.

As you are already aware, the Convention is a failure and the result was to be announced this week but the German's break through has upset it. The Convention a failure, Irish men being imprisoned at the rate of 21 a day, German marching through France, Ireland united now stands a chance of winning her freedom. 'Now or never' is the cry of Sinn Féin and I may tell you that England cannot humbug us much longer, the people won't have it. This in an age of freedom and well England knows it and in a few months more with God's help we will see the tricolour flying – the sign of a nation's freedom. There is now 1,400 Sinn Féin clubs in Ireland, not counting America, Australia, England and Scotland. In Cavan county we have 65, so you see, we are well organised and getting ready for the general election which must be fought under the new franchise and this will give us a large number of votes, in fact we expect to be able to turn about 65 candidates out of 90 and if we do, it means that England will have her hands full for a while and perhaps her jails too but we don't mind jail now.

The one word on every lip, the one burning in every heart, the one thing that animates and fires each Irish man today – Freedom – with such a spirit with such determination, England can fill her jails but while in jail or out, the ideal remains the same with this alteration - go into jail a lover of Ireland and you come out a hater of England. If you could see Ireland today, if you could see our meetings, if you could see our processions – all I can say is – a bright smile must light the face of Ireland's martyrs as today, they beside God's white throne, see the ideal for which they suffered and died for realised.

Now a word about home. Father and all are fine but no sign of Jimmy getting tied yet. How is my sheep getting along? It looks as if it won't be long till I see them now as it cannot be long until the war ends. You will perhaps be puzzled to know why I am so anxious to go but consumption during my term in prison has set in, in the back and I am afraid that the number of years I have to work on Ireland's cause is few, but if I live to see the Republican flag float and free and independent Ireland, I will willingly bow my head before the will of the divine providence. Father, Jimmy, Jonnie, Ellen, Paddy join in sending their love.

With fondest love from you affectionate brother,

Paul

P.S. Sometimes we have been getting all the papers you sent but no letters, it seems an age since I last got a letter from you but in this matter perhaps it is my own fault. I had a thousand messages to send you but like all mad Sinn Féiners forgot them.

With love from Paul

§   §   §

Letter 14 – From Paul Galligan to his girlfriend Mollie Coyle (later to be his wife)

Place of Internment: Reading Jail

19th December 1918

My Dear Mollie,

One thousand thanks for your very kind congratulations on West Cavan victory and I am glad to be able to return the compliment to East Cavan. Yes Mollie, Cavan has been a surprise to us all and as Napoleon would say 'it has covered itself with glory' and in future we can hold our heads high, 'Cavan is the gap of the North' and the lead that Cavan has given will be nobly followed by Ulster and some of the Ulster results will surprise even you Mollie.

I was very very sorry to hear that this awful pestilence which the English language calls 'flu' visited your home and it was sad to see all except my Bridie laid up and I am delighted to hear that it has passed over and that all are on their feet once more, but I expect a little weak still, but everyone should be most careful for a time yet, as it is in a relapse all the danger is. Well Mollie, I'm afraid there is more than Mr. Davys in love for you wrote 'St. Stephen's Night' for Halloween. I'm afraid I will have to write to your father and give him the symptoms.

Yes Mollie, the boys did enjoy that night and often they speak of it still but we are going to eclipse it on Christmas night and the decorations will I can assure you be more up to date. In fact we are all looking forward to it with a light heart and preparations have commenced already and in the next letter I will give you all news of the festivity. I am glad to hear that Miss O'Reilly reciprocates (oh, get a dictionary Mollie for those MP's are the devil for using big words) Mr. Davys good feeling. So God help me if it does not come. She will have to keep him with her now or I will not ask him to Cavan.

Anyway, I am doing the best I can and the photo will do the rest and of course I must be best man. We all expected to be with you long ago as it was almost certain that we would be released in the end of November but we have made up our minds for a few more months of prison life so by then you will be in good form to have my first speech. I believe you cut a great dash in Kilnarick Fair on December 4th. By the time you get this you will have had a good long chat with Nora. I pity the poor fellow that has crossed your path. Now Goodbye Mollie and I wish you all a very bright and happy Christmas. With love to Father, Mother, brothers and sisters and self.

Paul.

P.S. Mollie dear, on Christmas morning when you are at Mass I will ask you not to forget the poor exiles here and to say a special prayer for me and I will not forget you.

P.P.S. Mollie, I really feel ashamed of all your goodness. You are not right on your feet then you start sending parcels. The last two arrived safely and in good condition. To all my friends convey my best wishes. Say I wish them all a very happy and joyful Christmas. Goodbye Mollie and enjoy yourself at Christmas in the wish of your old friend, Paul.

P.P.P.S. Did you get PC I sent you a week ago? Give my love to Bridie to whom I send the only Christmas gift I am allowed.

Letter 15 – From Paul Galligan to his brother Monsignor Eugene Galligan

Drumnalaragh
Ballinagh

9th October 1919

My Dear Brother,

The last letter I wrote to you was from Belfast jail over a month ago and since then I had to pass through some trying scams. A trumped up court marshal in which every iota of evidence was forgery and which sentenced me to 12 months with hard labour, but the worst was to come – I would not be allowed political treatment and was placed amongst criminals.

On August 15th, the Governor told me I was to receive criminal treatment – this after a week's consideration by the Masonic Prison Board. I said to the Governor 'this is a declaration of war and it is now a fight between you representing the British Government and I representing the Irish Government and the Irish will win'. On Friday, I refused to exercise with criminals and on Monday morning at 7 a.m. I was handed in some food to have and I asked the warden to remove it as I was not a criminal. At 10 a.m. I was brought before the Governor and charged with insubordination (1) refusing to exercise (2) to work. And my answer was that I would refuse to do anything, work or otherwise which would make me a criminal. He then ordered me three days bread and water and three days close confinement. To this I replied 'I protested against your treatment and your consideration of that protest is to inflict on me the extreme criminal penalty in your power. I now further protest against your criminal treatment by refusing to take criminal food'. After a hunger strike of 10 days in which everything was done to break me off and which everything a hellish mind would think of to tempt a hungry man was brought to bear on me, but in vain. On 27 August I was released for a month and during that month I worked night and day as I knew they would again arrest me. In this I was correct.

Getting off the train at Cavan after a Conference of the Ulster Representations at Omagh, two policemen waiting for me at the station and shadowed me to a friend's house. Fortunately some other important business called me away for an hour with the result that the house was raided by 20 police in my absence so I escaped for the present. At all counts another trip to Belfast jail.

Things are going well in Ireland and the few who have held out against the Sinn Féin policy is now turning over and subscribing genuinely to the Republican loan which will be a great success here. I'm sure you have heard that America has already subscribed £5 million to this fund. Day by day the Irish case is getting stronger. Day after day we are beating England into a corner from which there is no escape and by the time this reaches you, England will have made an offer of a settlement to us but she will find different staff to deal with than the Imperial putty which Ireland had been sending to England for some time.

Circumstances will not allow me to stay at home for long but all letters addressed here will find me alright. I don't know if I thanked you for the present of cheque, it was so good of you to send it and I can assure you, I fully appreciate it as we take no expenses for work we are doing and your cheque enables me to keep up the dignity of the position I now hold. No word from Jimmy since, or is his name ever mentioned here and father is still very bitter against him. It will take you when you return home to put matters right. Dáil Eireann (how I smile) is suppressed and so is all our papers for publishing prospectus of the Republican Loan so I cannot send you papers but I will send the flags as promised. Also, other information or cuttings as they come to hand. Don't forget but write often but as you know this is a time when we have little time to ourselves so forgive the frankness of my letters.

With love from Paul.

p.s. I forgot to remark that the police who swore against me in my court marshal never returned to their barracks or have they been seen since. Again good-bye.

Bye, with love from Paul

 ❧   ❧   ❧

Letter 16 – From Paul Galligan to his brother Monsignor Eugene Galligan

Drumnalaragh
Ballinagh

19th December 1919

My Dear Brother,

I have just a few spare moments and I am going to drop you a few lines but it is very doubtful if they will reach you, but here goes. We are now living under a regime of terror, worst than even the Russians or Poles passed through when the Disposition of the Czar was at its worst. England today is a bi-word for the nations of the world. I just read today of her butchery in Ireland. England is manoeuvring for the same opportunity in Ireland but we know England's diplomacy too well by now.

The guillotine of Free Masonry in Ireland is being mounted once more but Sinn Féin refuses to put in its head. A Man of War that was to deport 400 Sinn Féiners to Warmound Prison outside of London which is wired to a height of 30 ft, guarded inside by soldiers and outside by police, sailed for London town with seven and their swoop which was to be a surprise is now the anger of Ireland but we expect another before the end of the week, but I am afraid the war ship will again remain empty. I am enclosing four clippings of late which may interest you. Since I refuse to report myself at Belfast the police have made seven raids for me, I enclose a short note on last one. Father is nearly all right again but Jonnie still complains. Good bye dear brother and remember us in your prayers. Father, Jonnie, Ellen and a host of your old friends join in wishing you a very happy and holy Christmas.

From your loving brother Paul.

Letter 17 – From Paul Galligan to his brother Monsignor Eugene Galligan

Drumnalaragh
Ballinagh, Co. Cavan

7 April 1920

My Dear Brother,

What a surprise to me to get a cheque for £100 a few days ago. It would be useless to try and thank you but I know the big heart you always possessed and in saying this perhaps you have deprived yourself of a well earned holiday. May God bless you is all I can say.

You must forgive me for not writing oftener but being in a position I am rarely ever appearing at home, it is hard to write as often as one would wish. Then all our letters being seized and opened by the authorities makes it much harder as we are uncertain what letters reach their destination. As well, the strain on each of us at present is terrific. Each man arrested means the transference of more work, but thank God we have strength and endurance to do it.

We are now preparing for the biggest fight of all – the County Councils. And as this election is being held under Proportional Representation it means an amount of extra work. It will be a wonderful test of our strength and by the time you get this letter, Ireland will have won the greatest victory. She will have chased out the old gang of selfish imperial crawlers and have replaced them by a body whose ambition is the prosperity of the country and who will not be afraid to do the right thing at the right time. The organisation for these elections is taking up all our time at present, as the selection of candidates, organising of staff, etc. is a big thing but when it is over, all Councils in Cavan will be Republican by a large majority.

I know what question is in your mind at this minute, what do we think of Home Rule? Well, as bad as we are now we would be a thousand times worse than we are at present. At present we all fight the most disproportionate rule, even worse than Poland and if we accepted Home Rule we would be accepting a proportion of this rule. Home Rule in a nut shell means a continuation of the present rule for under it we get nothing. England controls taxes, revenue, customs, post office, commerce, etc. We simply would be an Irish Parliament for gathering taxes. We tell her, gather her own taxes and pay for the gathering.

I heard no word from Jimmy for ages, why, I do not know. Father, Jonnie, Ellen are all keeping good considering their old age, all anxiously looking forward to your return. All the neighbours are good and all advancing in prosperity. Cattle and farm is paying well but foreign imports, meat, flour are going to be an awful price. I will now say goodbye and best love from all here.

From your loving brother

Paul.

§ § §

Letter 18 – From Paul Galligan to his father Peter Galligan

Liverpool Prison

28 October 1920

My Dear Dad,

At last I have the pleasure of writing to you from England. I hope you are fully recovered from your illness by now for I am afraid my arrest did not improve you and as no letter reached me lately, I am anxious about you all at home.

I got your letter which you sent to Belfast and the Governor there was kind enough to allow me a letter to reply and I had got no answer I am doubtful if it reached you. If not you will see that the deposits for £400 with interest is transferred to either the Hibernian or Provincial. I think I told you that I wrote to the manager of the Ulster a few days before my arrest notifying him of the withdrawal. I don't think, under the circumstances that he can make any objection, if so you can refer him to my letter. I think I paid up the insurance policy to April, if not you can see to what date and continue it until I return. To finish with money matters, I hope John got the message I sent to him from Belfast and Cavan regarding my accounts and if there is anything he cannot understand well it must wait till I see him myself, but I hope that he found money alright as there was a few items I forgot to explain but I hope he was able to put matters right. Tell him if he writes me a note and gives it to you to enclose that it will arrive alright.

Now how about you all – I know too well what a shock my arrest was, especially going away wounded. At any other time it would be bad enough but to come when I was most needed and you were so ill – but everything is in God's hands and I accept everything he sends for the best. I hope you are now back to your old self again. I was glad to hear that Dr. Clarke was able 'to work wonders' as you say yourself. He was very kind to me in Cavan and took infinite care in dressing my arm – indeed, I can never forget his kindness on that occasion. I am still in hospital and the arm is nearly alright again but a bit stiff as some of the muscles were severed but it will come alright with time.

My worst complaint is my old enemy, the stomach which is still making attacks on me and as a result I suffer a good deal from a pain in the head. The doctor here is very kind and attentive and I could not receive more attention or better care if I were at home.

I forgot to mention that the suitcase sent to Belfast arrived safely here and all articles of clothing, etc. were correct. Also, Blue Book which the Governor wrote for, has reached me. While in Cavan Police Barracks, Ms. Brady of Cavan House got me some collars, socks and tie as well as £5-10-0 in cash so the next time you are in Cavan you can have it settled up. How is things at home.

The weather has, with the exception of a few days (since I arrived here) is ideal and if you have the same in Ireland you are lucky. Have you got the same boy and girl yet? I know it is hard to keep your temper at times but still you will find it hard to get ones up to your own standard. However, you know best, but I am thinking of yourself, how hard it will be on you prowling around for servants. Give Joe and Kitty my regards. How is Jonnie and Ellen since I left? Poor Jonnie how I pitied him that day but it seems that the policeman was afraid of him as he took the fork from him. Many a time I have laughed at the incident since. How is the cattle doing? I expect you did not sell any since. Will you sell the bullock next month? I am anxious to know which of the black or white one brought the most money? The white one should have done well on the grass.

Had you any letter from Eugene lately as I was expecting one before my arrest. If one comes for me you can enclose it in your letter to me. You can tell him in your next that I will write as soon as possible and I send my love and he is not to forget me in his masses and prayers. We have the great consolation of being able to hear Mass every Sunday (as it is in very few prisons that Mass is said regularly on Sundays) and receive communion so I am quite happy and you need not worry about me. After Mass on Sunday the priest tells us the news of the week. It takes him about five minutes to give us this long waited for news which includes some Irish items. Though the Irish news is scanty still it is enough to show us what you are suffering and all that is left for us poor exiles is to pray for you all and this we do from our heart. In the silence of the night many a Rosary is offered up in the prison cells for poor old Ireland. Tell Fr. Mullin that I got his wire a few hours before I left Belfast for here and that I am grateful for his advice and that I have acted on it and at the first opportunity I will write him a long letter.

How is poor Tommy Fitz. I hope he is home by now, but I am afraid. Remember me to all the Ballinagh folk especially to Charles and Nora. There are a host of names I could write to be remembered to – give them all my love and say I am as happy as can be. Several letters sent here have been returned. If you meet anyone who has wrote and have this letter returned say I am sorry to be deprived of these kind messages. Now I want you to write me a long letter giving me all the news since I left. Let it be as long as possible, you don't know how I look forward to your letters. Tell John to write me and don't post yours until you get it. Again, give my regards to all my friends and love to Jonnie, Ellen and self.

From your loving son, Paul.

Letter 19 – Letter from Paul Galligan to his brother Monsignor Eugene Galligan

Lincoln Prison

2 March 1921

I would have written to you much sooner but watching a letter from you. I did not get your Christmas letter and the Governor told me that it arrived and that you intended writing latter. Well dear brother since I wrote you last there has been many changes. Yes, changes that have brought sorrow to many homes, especially to our own. When I left home father was just recovering from a severe stomach attack and his letters to me in Belfast and Liverpool were bright and cheery and he said he was alright again. What was my surprise after the transfer to here was a wire asking me to apply for parole as he was dying. I did so but being an Irish criminal I would not be allowed to see my dying father. This was the reply I received an hour before the wire announcing his death. Although I was prepared for it, still, it was a great shock to be cut off from all that the world holds dearest, in one blow, for he had been a father and a mother to me up to his death. The greater the trouble and the darker the clouds, the more kind he was.

As this letter had to pass through indifferent hands I cannot open my heart to you as a brother should to a brother. It would relieve me to be able to tell you my grief and trouble but it cannot be until the prison gates are left behind once more. Poor dad, how I miss you when that day comes. I will miss that bright smile of welcome and joy with which he always had when I returned home. It can never be home to me again. For all that wants to make it a home is gone. Here in my cell at night during those long dreary nights I keep thinking, thinking of him, how he must have felt during those last hours with not one of us to say goodbye. It was a hard cruel hand, but why should I grieve, his last hours were the happiest in his whole life and he died with that pure Irish Catholic prayer on his lips 'Jesus Mary and Joseph, help me'.

As there is no one at home now who can write, it is hard to get reliable news, so I'm unable to tell you anything regarding the old folk. I had a long kind and sympathetic letter from Nora (that is Sister Julian's sister) giving me all the details of funeral. This is the only letter I may say I had got relating to home. Letters are most unsatisfactory as it takes from three weeks to a month to get a reply. You are surrounded by a web of formalities and technicalities which your friends don't know, with the result that our letters are long overdue before they reach us.

I had a visit from Jimmy last month. It was a surprise as he was the last person in the world I expected to see. When I was called up and told my brother was to visit me, I thought it was you, but then I knew that was impossible. Not much changed since I saw him last which is three years ago – a bit stouter and has the farmer's look about him. He too was greatly cut up over father's death as he never expected it. As he had not been at home or heard from anyone, he could give me very little news. His visit lasted half an hour and I felt happy after seeing him as I was longing for someone I could speak with regarding home. He promised me he would go home as I am anxious about the old people as they have only strangers on whom to rely. I don't know if he has done so as I have got no reply as yet to my last letter which I wrote a month ago. But if he has gone home I expect he has written to you himself and given you all the home news.

I had a letter from Fr. Dolan who is curate in Drumkilly and who has taken a great interest in the old people as well as assisting them in all financial matters. He said that Johnny had got a bad cold after Christmas but was then on the road to recovery. Poor soul, it is a pity to see him suffer and I hope Jimmy has gone home to relieve him of the heavy burden which has fallen on his shoulders.

I expect you are anxious to hear about myself. I expect father sent you all the details of my arrest. The wound which I got was only a slight one in the wrist. The bullet when passing through the arm severed some of the sinews and it will take time before it will be right, but I can use it except lifting heavy weights – then it pains. What I suffer most from is the stomach and nerves since my imprisonment. I may say, I have been all the time under the Doctor's care and have put four months in hospital. Very little can be done for me while I am in here as the confinements and environment is against me and I am afraid I will have to undergo an operation immediately upon my release. I was told by a Dublin specialist that I would have no relief until this was done but the dreaded horror of an operation prevented me from doing so until too late.

I have only three months more of my year to do and with God's help, I won't find it passing and a few months of the pure Irish air will work wonders. After leaving Belfast jail, our first destination was Liverpool prison where after 12 weeks we were again moved to here and 'here we are'. I was sorry leaving Liverpool prison as we had just settled down to the prison routine. On arriving here, we found we were the only Catholic prisoners and could not have Mass. We felt this very much as we had prayers during three mornings of the week and Mass at 9 on Sunday and benediction at 1.30 in Liverpool. For six weeks we had no Mass and this I felt worst of all. For what is work and what is imprisonment when you can receive the blessed sacrament. We now have mass every Tuesday morning and we are quite happy. When I come back to my cell on Tuesday morning after Mass with communion I feel real happy for kneeling on the bare cell floor with your little crucifix hanging on the wall in front. You really feel that you are nearer to God than out in the busy material world. Yes, we are happy.

In Nora's letter she said you stated in one of your wires to father that you intended coming home this year. If you have not made arrangements before this reaches you I would advise you to postpone your visit until next year as there is no one at home to make the necessary preparations. As well, your visit would be hampered by the many restrictions that are in force at present and motoring is not only dangerous but impossible owing to the state of the roads. Next year things will be brighter and you can enjoy your well earned holiday in a land where the air will be pure and free. As I expect to be leaving here by the end of June, you should not write to this address but to home as I expect to be there when your reply arrives. There are many things I would like to say but for the present must remain unsaid otherwise you would not get this. If you are writing to Sister Julian, please remember me to her and ask her to remember me in her prayers. For the present I will say goodbye – dear brother and don't worry about me as I am happy. I would ask you to remember me in your prayers and sometimes in your Masses.

God bless you and guard you.
With best love from your fond brother Paul

P.S. I had not the pleasure of receiving the last letters you addressed to me at home. Father enclosed them in his letter to me in Liverpool, but as they contained news of a political nature, I did not get them, but I expect to receive them on my release. Again good-bye and again God bless you, Paul.

Letter 20 – From Paul Galligan to his brother Monsignor Eugene Galligan

Lincoln Prison
England

29th May 1921

My Dear Brother,

At last I had the privilege of receiving a letter of March 25th. It reached me over a fortnight ago. I need not tell you what joy it was as I had given up hope of hearing from you while here. I wrote to you about 1 March and I hope it reached you safely. I would have written to you earlier, only Nora Fitzpatrick in writing after father's death, said she had sent you on my letter and since then I have been watching, watching for a letter. As each letter came due I thought of writing to you but always postponing it expecting to have word before my next letter came along and while I was waiting to avoid, occurred both writing together. 'Sorrow never comes alone' is an old proverb and in our case, alas a true one.

Since you wrote, poor Uncle Jonnie has passed to his reward. Poor soul. I feel his loss almost as much as fathers for has he not been more than a father to us all? Indeed, no father could do more than he and during those early years when we were under his charge and to the end he thought of nothing else but our interests. Since his death I often think of the winter evening when all were gathered around the fire listening to the paper being read and his humours or biting comments on the news, especially those events of later days. His life was a pure and spotless one and his death holy and sanctified. I know you will always remember him in your prayers and his memory next to fathers will be forever treasured in my heart.

You were quite right when you say that prison gives you greater scope for 'brooding'. The rigid discipline, the enforcement of a strict silence will effect iron nerves and soon lead you to sad and melancholy thoughts. God gave to each and every one of us a brain, the most perfect of all his handwork - in which originates those great and lofty ideas, those pure and noble thoughts and a tongue to express, expand and develop them, but the laws of man say that the tongue must remain silent, the brain dormant.

When news of father's death reached me I was suffering from acute gastritis and had no sleep for a number of nights. Father's death had its effect for I felt I was going mad and such were the awful fits of depression and despondency, that I would have welcomed madness as a relief. No one holds the greater horror of suicide as I do, but looking back on my experience, my horror is turned to pity. For those who don't believe in a hereafter, suicide is a relief from some of the agonies we are called upon to endure. Yes, prison is the hardest place of all to hear that our nearest and dearest is dead. No kind word to cheer you on – no consoling word to give you hope and sympathy, but the deadly silence of your cell, no one could express it better than O'Donovan Rossa: 'The news of death is saddening even in the festive hall / When heard through prison bars it is saddest of them all.'

I told you in my last letter that I had a visit from Jimmy in the end of February before he went home. Since then I have heard from him at regular periods and it seems as if things at home are going along smoothly. I notice by your letter that you are not satisfied with his conduct. In this we are of one mind, but I too have suspended my judgement until he can give a satisfactory explanation and it is only fair and reasonable that he would be allowed this.

As Fr. Dolan, who attended father has written to you I expect he has told you that I am to succeed to the property. I regret this for you as you know I had made up my mind to a commercial life as I never was in love with farming, but fate seems to have tied me to it. During father's last illness before I left home I approached him about a reconciliation with Jimmy but he would not listen. I told him that (as he knew) that I intended starting in business at an early date and then Jimmy should come home and help him. He then said that all was willed to me and if I did not accept it, to tell him then as he would will it to the others, his own words being 'Don't compel me Paul to hand this place over to strangers'. I promised to remain and look after the old couple. He then said 'I am satisfied now'. Only for making this promise it is doubtful that I would ever go home for all that helped me to make it bright and cheery has passed away. However, I must face it and that is why I am glad you have suspended judgement also, that justice may be done to Jimmy.

I had a letter for Patrick's day from Teresa in which she said she had wrote to you and was watching for a reply. She is a real good soul and is by far the best of the family. I got my letters regular and all the local news. Of course political items are strictly censored and I am as ignorant of Irish events as the man in the moon. I will be a regular Rip-Van-Winkle as regards Ireland when I leave here. I know that like Rip, I will rub my eyes when I see some of the changes. Where I once saw happy homes I will see blackened ruins if not worse.

Well brother, this is my last letter from Lincoln Prison and long before it has reached you I hope to be back in dear old Ireland, back to the pure air of the hills. There is nothing certain in prison life but I am due for release on this day fortnight, that is 11th June. Since my imprisonment I have suffered again from a stomach and at present the nerves are in a deplorable state. I expect to reach Dublin on Sunday morning and if possible make arrangements to see a specialist on Monday. I am determined not to lose an hour until I have a specialist's opinion for I feel myself that it is serious and I will have to arrange an operation and as soon as it is over the better. Owing to the present state of the nerves, I may be compelled to take a rest before an operation can be performed. If this is so, I will go home first and settle up some legal matters and then if I can get a quiet nook along the sea I will enjoy a rest. Soon you can write home and if I am not there they can send this along.

Before this reaches you, Archbishop Mannix will have returned to Australia without seeing the home of his childhood or the land of his breath. What petty persecution from those who believe in a 'free constitution' and 'The Great Charter of Freedom'. What an answer to the cry 'Fight for Catholic Belgium'. It is only an honour postponed some day in the near future we will welcome him back to a new Ireland to crown him with prayers, tears and love. The most precious gifts in our power.

One thousand thanks for your kindness of which I had many tokens in the past. Now that father is dead we are still bound together by a closer link and I shall look to you in the future for that advice which he would give. God bless you for your kind consoling letter it did more than all other letters which I have received, it helped 'to make the heavy load lighter and the dark road brighter'. Don't forget to write to me often for your letters always bring me comfort and conciliation so I will be anxiously looking forward to them. I will now say goodbye and I will again ask you to remember me always in your prayers.

With best love from your fond brother.

Paul

Letter 21 – From Paul Galligan to his brother Monsignor Eugene Galligan

(no address and not prison paper)

30 June 1921

My Dear Brother,

I am sure you are anxious to know how I am getting along since I left Lincoln. I wrote you a week before I left that hospitable concern and again a few days before I left Liverpool and I hope those letters reached you safely. If you got my Liverpool letter it will explain my last letter from Lincoln and I am glad to say it's succeeded as I am now on Irish soil once more and away in a cosy corner on the coast enjoying the invigorating air of my native land. I have not yet visited home as I did not think it wise to do so for they would certainly be on the alert and, as well, a rest was essential. I am quite happy here and if I had anyone I knew it would be heaven but I expect some friends along this week to brighten things a bit.

I have written indirectly to Jimmy but as yet got no reply as I am anxious to know how things are at home but his last letter was encouraging and I hope he will be able to keep going. I expect you are all anxious for Irish news but I am sorry I cannot give you much as I have as yet not got in touch with my colleagues. Here in an isolated part I find it hard to get in touch and harder still to take up the threads where I left them ten months ago.

By now the Press of the world is commenting on Lloyd George's letter to our President. To meet him in a conference in 10 Downing Street to come to a final settlement. As a preliminary, Dev has asked the Unionists of North and South to meet him in Dublin on Monday next so that a united Ireland should decide her own fate. The orange Premier has refused which shows that he is acting according to London. He got a glorious chance to stand by Ireland but he has thrown it away and he shall live to regret it. The humblest Unionist sees that his parliament is a fiasco – worse is a financial bankrupt and a new feeling is sweeping over Ulster and it is that if Ulster must be prosperous there must be only one parliament. The result you will know long before this reaches you but it is in God's hands and he will in his own time crown the Irish nation with liberty.

I will write to you as often as possible but as I am still cut off from official sources I have very little to write. In the event of hearing information of final settlement I will wire it to you.

Goodbye and write to me at home address as often as possible,

Best love from your fond brother Paul

Bibliography

Primary Sources

The most important source for this book is the personal correspondence of Paul Galligan, mostly between him and his brother Eugene. These letters are in the possession of the Galligan family, kindly lent to the author by Máirín Dillon (née Galligan).

UK National Archives, Kew, England

Intrigues Between Sinn Féin Leaders and the German Government, CAB/24/117, The National Archives, Kew, Richmond, Surrey, TW9 4DU, England.

Daily Police Reports, 1916 Rebellion, WO 35/69/1, The National Archives, Kew, Richmond, Surrey, TW9 4DU, England.

Speech Notes Recorded by the Police, CO 904/23/3, The National Archives, Kew, Richmond, Surrey, TW9 4DU, England.

Castle File No. 88, GALLIGAN, Peter Paul, WO 35/207, The National Archives, Kew, Richmond, Surrey, TW9 4DU, England.

County Inspector's Report, 1919, CO 904/109, The National Archives, Kew, Richmond, Surrey, TW9 4DU, England.

Bureau of Military History Archive (BMH) (Located at Military Archives, Cathal Brugha Barracks, Dublin 6.)

Witness Statement, Peter Paul Galligan, WS 170, 17 December 1948.

Peter Paul Galligan Collection [CD 105].

Cavan

Witness Statement Seamus MacDiarmada, WS 768, 1 December 1952.

Witness Statement Seamus McKenna, WS 1,016, 6 October 1954.

Witness Statement, Francis Connell, WS 1,663, 28 August 1957.

Witness Statement, James Cahill WS 503, 11 April 1951.

Witness Statement, Bernard Brady, WS 1,626, 4 June 1957.

Witness Statement by Seán Sheridan, WS 1,613, 9 May 1957.

Witness Statement Hugh Maguire, WS 1,387, 28 March 1956.

Witness Statement, Peadar McMahon, WS 1,730, 5 October 1955.

Wexford

Witness Statement, Seamus Doyle, WS 215 (Easter Rising), 12 October 1949 and WS 1,342 (Dartmoor) 25 January 1956.

Witness Statement, Thomas Dwyer, WS 1,198, 20 June 1955.

Witness Statement, James J. O'Connor, WS 1,214, 27 July 1955.

Witness Statement, Patrick Ronan, WS 299, 14 October 1949.

Witness Statement, James Cullen, WS 1,343, 25 January 1956.

Witness Statement John J. O'Reilly, WS 1,031, 25 October 1954.

Witness Statement, Mrs Richard Mulcahy/Mary Josephine Mulcahy (Ryan), WS 399, 23 June 1950.

Witness Statement, Fr. Patrick Murphy, WS 1216, 22 July 1955.

Witness Statement, James Gleeson, WS 1,012, 18 September, 1954.

Witness Statement, Patrick Fitzpatrick, WS 1,274, 10 October 1955.

Note: In addition to the Witness Statements listed above, the author also sought Witness Statements for the individuals listed below, but they were not available: Seamus Rafter, J.J. 'Ginger' O'Connell, Seán Etchingham, Teddy Brosnan, Eoin MacNeill, Brennan Whitmore, Robert Brennan, Mollie Coyle, Seán Sinnott, Seán Milroy and Paul McShane.

University College Dublin Archive

Peter Paul Galligan Papers [P25], Archives Department, UCD, Dublin 4.

Newspapers and Magazines

Irish Freedom 1910-1914, National Library of Ireland.

The Anglo-Celt, Cavan, Saturday 25 August 1917, Page 2.

The Anglo-Celt, Cavan, Saturday 11 September 1920, Page 1.

The Irish Times, Dublin, 14 August 1919, Page 6.

The Irish Times, Dublin, 6 September 1919, Page 8.

New York Times, 15 December 1922.

Secondary Sources

Books

Abbott, Richard, *Police Casualties in Ireland, 1919-1921*, Mercier, 2002.

Andrews, Todd, *Dublin Made Me*, Lilliput Press, Dublin 2002.

Bartlett, Thomas, Jeffrey, Keith, *A Military History of Ireland*, Cambridge University Press 1997.

Carlyle, Thomas, *The French Revolution*, Abridged and Edited, by A.H.R Ball, Cambridge 1930.

Campbell, Fergus, *Land and Revolution: Nationalist Politics in the West of Ireland 1891-1921*, Oxford University Press, Oxford, 2008.

Coleman, Marie, *County Longford and the Irish Revolution 1910-1923*, Irish Academic Press, Dublin 2006.

Collins, M.E., *Ireland 1868-1968*, The Educational Company of Ireland, Dublin 1993.

Coogan, Tim Pat, *Michael Collins*, Arrow Books, London, 1991.

Coogan, Tim Pat, *1916, The Easter Rising*, Phoenix, London 2005.

Coogan, Tim Pat, *De Valera*, Hutchinson, London, 1993.

Coogan, Tim Pat, *Ireland in the Twentieth Century*, Hutchinson, The Random House Group Limited, 2003.

Doherty, Gabriel, Keogh, Dermot (eds.), *1916 – The Long Revolution*, Mercier Press, Cork 2007.

Dwyer, Ryle T., *Tans, Terror and Troubles: Kerry's Real Fighting Story*, Mercier Press, Cork, 2001.

Fitzgerald, Desmond, *The Memoirs of Desmond Fitzgerald*, Routledge & Keegan Paul, London 1968.

Ferriter, Diarmaid, *Judging Dev: A Reassessment of the Life and Legacy of Eamon de Valera*, Royal Irish Academy, Dublin 2007.

Garvin, Tom, *The Evolution of Irish Nationalist Politics* (1981), Gill & Macmillan, Dublin 2005.

Gialanella Valiulis, Maryann, *Portrait of a Revolutionary General: Richard Mulcahy and the Founding of the Irish Free State*, Irish Academic Press, Dublin, 1992.

Goff, Henry, *Wexford Has Risen*, Co. Wexford 1916 Trust Ltd, 2007.

Hart, Peter, *The IRA and its Enemies: Violence and Community in Cork 1916-1923*, Clarendon Press, Oxford 1999.

Hart, Peter, *Mick, The Real Michael Collins*, Macmillan, 2006.

Hopkinson, Michael, *Green Against Green: The Irish Civil War*, Gill & Macmillan, Dublin 2004.

Hopkinson, Michael, *The Irish War of Independence*, Gill & Macmillan, Dublin 2004.

Kostick, Conor & Collins, Lorcan, *The Easter Rising: A Guide to Dublin in 1916*, The O'Brien Press Limited, 2000.

Laffan, Michael, *The Resurrection of Ireland: The Sinn Féin Party, 1916-1923*, Cambridge University Press, 2000.

Lynch, Robert, *Northern Divisions*: *The Northern IRA and the Early Years of Partition*, Irish Academic Press, Dublin 2006.

Mac Atasney, Gerard, *Seán MacDiarmada: The Mind of a Revolution*, Drumlin 2004.

McGarry, Fearghal, *Eoin O'Duffy: A Self-Made Hero*, Oxford University Press, Oxford, 2007.

McGarry, Fearghal, *The Rising: Ireland Easter 1916*, Oxford University Press, Oxford 2010.

Maguire, Commandant Hugh, *After Easter 1916*, Black & Co. Printers, Cavan, 1956.

Philpin, Charles, H.E, *Nationalism and Popular Protest in Ireland*, Cambridge University Press, 2002.

Sheehan, William, *Hearts and Mines: The British 5th Division in Ireland 1920-1922*, Collins, Dublin 2009.

Sullivan T. (ed.), *Drumkilly: From Ardkill Mountain to Kilderry Hill*, Drumkilly History Committee, Cavan 2000.

Townshend Charles, *Easter 1916 – The Irish Rebellion*, Penguin, London 2006.

Regan, John M, *The Irish Counter Revolution 1921-1931: Treatyite Politics and Settlement In Independent Ireland*, Gill & MacMillan, 1999.

Walker, Brian M. (ed.) *Parliamentary Election Results in Ireland 1801–1922*. Dublin: Royal Irish Academy, 1978.

Online Resources

National Census Archive 1901, http://www.census.nationalarchives.ie/pages/1901/Cavan/Derrin/Drumnalaragh/

The 1918 Election results: http://www.ark.ac.uk/elections/h1918.htm

Ida Milne, Is History Repeating? The Spanish flu of 1918 http://puesoccurrences.com/2009/06/02/history-repeating-the-spanish-flu-of-1918/

Hammar Greenwood on 'Murders in Ireland', 16 June, 1921 (HC Deb 16 June 1921 vol 143 cc571-4) http://hansard.millbanksystems.com/commons/1921/jun/16/murders

T.C. Maguire, N.T, Breifne Journal of Cumann Seánchais Bhreifne (Breifne Historical Society) Volume IV No 14 (1971)

http://www.stpeter.utvinternet.com/headstones-print.htm

Dáil debates: Located at http://debates.oireachtas.ie/Dail

Cavan IRA memorial, Cavan Courthouse: Picture and inscription at http://commons.wikimedia.org/wiki/File:Cavan_courthouse_statue.jpg

Election results for Cavan, 1922 and 1923:
(a)http://electionsireland.org/result.cfm?election=1923&cons=36
(b) http://electionsireland.org/result.cfm?election=1922&cons=36
Walsh, Robert, Dartmoor, 'The Prison that broke the Body and then the Soul', *Crime Magazine*, 16 May 2010, http://crimemagazine.dreamhosters.com/dartmoor-prison-broke-body-and-then-soul

Index